Road Runner

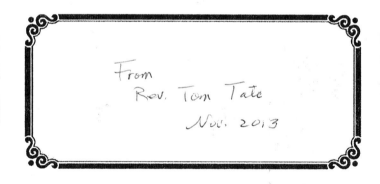

From
Rev. Tom Tate
Nov. 2013

Thomas G. Bandy

Road Runner

The Body in Motion

Abingdon Press
Nashville

ROAD RUNNER
THE BODY IN MOTION

Copyright © 2002 by Abingdon Press

This book is printed on recycled, acid-free paper.

Library of Congress Cataloging-in-Publication Data

Bandy, Thomas G., 1950-
  Road runner : the body in motion / Thomas G. Bandy.
    p. cm. — (The convergence eBook series)
  ISBN 0-687-02174-X (pbk. : alk. paper)
  1. Church renewal. I. Title. II. Series.
  BV600.3 .B37 2002
  250—dc21

2002006641

02 03 04 05 06 07 08 09 10 11—10 9 8 7 6 5 4 3 2 1

MANUFACTURED IN THE UNITED STATES OF AMERICA

CONTENTS

WARM UP

I am a "road runner." I spend between 200 and 230 days a year traveling by road, rail, air, and occasionally water, pursuing my mission to help other Christian leaders pursue their missions. Along the way there are many unexpected mishaps and surprising opportunities. Recently I left home having packed three changes of clothes, and was gone two weeks.

One of these unexpectedly long trips involved a consultation with a group of denominational judicatory leaders. I decided I needed a new pair of shoes, and ran over to one of those big "box stores" that sell sports apparel. I was looking for sneakers, and discovered that they do not make them anymore. Instead there were walking shoes, tennis shoes, rugby shoes, golf shoes, skateboarding shoes, joggers, runners, and cross-trainers. I not only had to choose between a bewildering array of brand names, I had to decide among cushioned heels, airflow soles, synthetic materials, high-tops and low-tops, and treads. "All I want is a pair of sneakers," I said to the salesman. All I got was a thirty-minute lecture on the science of shoe design.

I found myself wondering: When did the simple act of running become an institution? It used to be that if a body wanted to run, he or she simply stepped out of the house, sniffed the wind, and set off down the road. Now it seems that a body needs to research running databases on the Web, shop the stores, watch a video, and train for ten weeks.

I also found myself wondering: When did the simple act of walking down the Emmaus road to catch up to Jesus in the mission field become a denomination? It used to be that if a disciple wanted to run, he or she simply stepped out of the inn, sniffed the spirit, and set off down the highway. Now it seems that a body needs to research the history of ministry, become certified, and file a strategic plan.

Actually, I think it happened this way.

I think a bunch of disciples gathered in the inn on the road to Emmaus in hopes of catching up to the risen Christ who had already resumed his journey down the road. Before they set out, somebody began asking questions. What kind of roads will they experience? Will it be wet? Will it be dusty? Will it be slippery? What kind of shoes should they wear? How fast is Jesus going? Should they wear runners, joggers, or walkers? After all, they didn't want to become crippled at a crucial moment of the mission, or fall down simply because they were inadequately equipped. So the disciples started debating the virtues of "Vibram" soles and leather uppers, and soon there were vehement arguments, and innovative shoe designs, and multiple brand names.

Then just as they were about to depart well shod, someone started asking other questions. What if one of us gets lost? Who will go look for him? What if someone falls behind? Who will wait for him? What if someone is attacked by bandits? Who will perform the rescue? What if Jesus takes a sudden turn, and we miss him along the way? How will we know? Should we have an oversight committee? Should we provide adequate health care? A pension plan? A guaranteed appointment? Should we send a bishop or a moderator farther down the road to scout the territory?

Then, just as they were about to depart well organized, someone started asking more questions. What if others come to the inn looking for us, and do not know where we have gone? What if they fail to wear the right shoes? What if they do not know the intricate science of putting one foot in front of the other, shifting their weight from heel to toe, balancing the head between squared shoulders, and walking with just the right bounce to their step?

In the end, I think these disciples postponed running down the road indefinitely and opened a big shoe store at the intersection of the Emmaus road and Interstate 95. And that is how the simple act of running became a denomination.

It is said that fewer than 1 percent of the people who buy sports shoes actually play tennis, basketball, or rugby, or actually walk, jog, run, or cross-train. They just wear the shoes, pose in coffee bars as if they had not really driven to get there, show up occasionally to use the treadmill at the local fitness center, and argue vehemently about brand names. One can easily speculate that fewer than 1 percent of the church members in North American denominations actually run after Jesus on the road to Emmaus as disciples. Most just wear the shoes, pose on church boards as if they had not really just been guilt-tripped to fill an office, show up occasionally to use the liturgy in Sunday worship, and argue vehemently about brand names.

Yet the more I travel among Christian leaders, the more I see a restlessness emerging. There is more and more curiosity about the Emmaus road, more and more impatience with the shoe store, and more and more enthusiasm to be wherever it is that Jesus went. This book is for those people. It is for people who simply can no longer keep still. It is for people who want to be moving—walking, jogging, skipping, marching, or running—to be with Jesus way beyond Emmaus. The chapters are designed to help you open your eyes, open your ears, open your minds, open your hearts, and open your doors so that you can set out on this great adventure.

Chapter 1, "The Road to Mission," opens your eyes to the contemporary pagan world, and contrasts the decline of official Christian religion with the emergence of the Christian movement.

Chapter 2, "The Body in Motion," contrasts the two fundamental choices facing people at the close of the modern age, Gnosticism and the Way of Christ. Standing smugly still with hidden knowledge, or traveling the unknown in the companionship of Jesus are the emerging choices replacing old stereotypes of "evangelical" and "mainstream" denominations. These choices are separating stagnant spiritualities based on personal privilege from vital movements bringing welcome relief to ordinary people.

Chapter 3, "The Heart of the Matter," opens your hearts to rehabilitate the "body of Christ" to follow Jesus into mission through a fat-free diet, rigorous exercise, and sound stress management. The "Vitality diet" enables the body of Christ to resist or recover from "heart disease," spiritual aerobics helps the body find its health in mission, and devotion focus reduces stress.

Chapter 4, "O Brother, Where Art Thou?" asks the postmodern version of the ancient question *Quo Vadis?* It invites a lifestyle that leaves official Christian religion behind to follow Jesus in mission to the contemporary pagan world.

The truth is that the institutional church in North America is in very serious trouble. Most of the people wearing running shoes today are overweight, out of shape, and no longer credible athletes in the spiritual competition of the pagan world. Providentially, just when it seems institutional churches are dropping out of the race, a new generation of Christian disciples is hitting the open road.

One

THE ROAD TO MISSION

The "body of Christ" is a body in movement. The great mistake of Christendom since the time of Constantine is that church leaders have misrepresented the body of Christ as passive. They imagine the body to be a body at rest. They think that the victory over paganism has been won, and that the body of Christ simply needs to consolidate that victory by erecting cathedrals, writing curricula, developing polities, and ordaining clergy. They interpret the body of Christ as an organization with rules, elected or appointed leaders, members, obligations, and secret handshakes. The great mistake is in believing that the pagan world is gone, and that the body is most visible when sitting in the pews of a sanctuary at worship. In reality, the body of Christ is in a perpetual state of unrest. It is traveling into the mission field of the pagan world.

The Acts of the Apostles and the Epistles constitute the travelogue of a body in movement. The key stories are all "road stories." Christ is always appearing while disciples are on the way to somewhere. Decisive insights and revelations are always happening in between destinations.

- Paul experiences Jesus on the Damascus road.
- Philip encounters the Ethiopian financier on the Gaza road.

- The faithful are "scattered abroad" from Jerusalem "preaching Christ" (see Acts 8:4, 5).
- Peter leaves abruptly to meet Cornelius in Joppa.
- Barnabas, Paul, Silas, Apollos, and many others travel by land and sea across the empire.

This image of the body in movement (not in stasis) is the whole point of Luke's story of the road to Emmaus (Luke 24). Paul's companion in the mission to the Gentiles is the only Gospel writer to tell the story. It is a mistake to consider this story yet another resurrection narrative. There are already plenty of these stories, and if you do not yet believe that Christ is risen, then one more story won't help. Luke tells the story of the Emmaus road because it is a mission story. The person and work of Jesus are tied to the mission of Jesus. The risen Lord is on his way somewhere, and is constrained by the disciples to stay for dinner at the wayside inn. There he is revealed in his true identity, and immediately disappears. The logical question is "Where did he go?" Surely, he returned to the journey that was his original purpose. He is on the road to Emmaus, away from Jerusalem, to the places where the Gentiles are.

Luke does not tell this story as another proof of the resurrection of Jesus. Luke tells this story as another proof of the stupidity of Jesus' disciples. They are human. They are addicted to any number of self-destructive personal and corporate habits that could have affected anyone else in their day as they do in this day. The incredible stupidity of the disciples—the amazing obtuseness, the astonishing lack of discernment—is that when they realize that this strange person who makes their hearts burn within them is indeed Jesus, and that Jesus is on the road to Emmaus, they go in the opposite direction and return to Jerusalem! Admittedly, they want to tell the other disciples that Jesus is alive, and that Jesus is on the road to Emmaus. Nevertheless, their behavior astonishes even Luke. If you had met the risen Lord, and if the risen Lord had made your heart burn within you, and if you knew where the risen Lord was going, *wouldn't you want to go with him?* Why on earth would you return to the head office in Jerusalem? Luke later tells how the apostles finally set out on the road to follow Jesus, and how it took until Acts 15 for them to catch up. They wanted to be with Jesus, and Jesus was no longer in Jerusalem with the denominational franchise. He was on the road to the spiritually yearning, institutionally alienated public.

The Christian "Road Runner"

Traditional interpreters of Paul's Epistle to the Philippians claim that Paul's central metaphor here is that of a foot race. They suggest that Paul is thinking of the relay races so popular in the sports arenas, in which the baton is passed from runner to runner until the last runner wins the crown of victory. This is a very convenient interpretation especially if the church really pictures itself as a passive body of Christ cheering the runners on and celebrating the victory later surrounded by the "fixed assets" of the cathedral. Yet this interpretation does not do justice to the mobility that was the central feature of Paul's own life.

> Three times I was shipwrecked; for a night and a day I was adrift at sea; on frequent journeys, in danger from rivers, danger from bandits, danger from my own people, danger from Gentiles, danger in the city, danger in the wilderness, danger at sea, danger from false brothers and sisters; in toil and hardship, through many a sleepless night, hungry and thirsty, often without food, cold and naked. (2 Cor. 11:25b-27)

Paul is emphasizing not just the dangers of his mission, but also the constant urgency and mobility of his life. He is preeminently a traveler, the very image of a body in movement. When Paul hopes that in the day of Christ he will discover that he has "not run in vain" (Phil. 2:16), it is more likely that he is hoping that all that travel by land and sea across the known world has not been wasted. If his life is a "foot race," it is best understood as a life of constant movement, the only real reward for which is to arrive safe and sound at one's destination. Who awaits Paul to embrace him at his final destination? It is Jesus, of course, who first launched himself down the road to Emmaus so long ago (Phil. 3:14).

Paul perceives the body of Christ as a body in movement. He compares this body to the "road runners" who traveled perpetually and extensively and at some risk all across the known world. Residents of the Roman Empire traveled constantly. In fact, it would be the nineteenth century before the region encompassed by the Roman Empire of the first century again experienced such extensive travel![1] Paul probably traveled about ten thousand miles sharing the roads and seas with "government officials, traders, pilgrims, the sick, letter-carriers, sightseers, runaway slaves, fugitives, prisoners, athletes, artisans, teachers, and students."[2] All this movement was quite miraculous in a culture in which mobility among social classes was so limited. The infrastructure of roads and shipping routes, combined with the Roman "peace" that made travel relatively safe from bandits, transformed early Christianity. Rather than becoming a temple, the church became a way station; it catapulted Christians out of the role of priests, and into that of road runners.

When you think of the body of Christ, Paul says, do not imagine that this is a body at rest, surrounded by lovely possessions, familiarly at ease with the surrounding microculture, greeted with knowing nods by passing neighbors.

- Imagine instead a body in movement, walking or running down well-paved roads, among people traveling by donkey, horse, chariot, automobile, or bus, mingling, talking, trading, sharing news, including the best news ever, Jesus Christ. Travel the "common route" across Asia Minor from Ephesus, up the Maeander Valley, through Antioch and Tarsus, all the way to the Euphrates or Mississippi Rivers. Travel the Via Egnatia from Greece, across the mountains to Heraclea, Edessa, and the primary ports of Philippi, Neapolis, or New York. Imagine sitting in wayside inns with imperial messengers and truck drivers, or pausing for a year in a convenient microculture or tribe to establish a Christian community, before moving on to the next microculture or tribe.

- Imagine instead a body in movement, sailing a hundred miles a day, constantly measuring the degree of urgency against the risks of stormy weather. Sometimes the traveler could ride the big grain ships from Alexandria to Rome, mingling with soldiers and prisoners being taken on appeal to Rome, and other "linear thinkers" following the straight course of a strategic plan. Sometimes the traveler would ride in small craft, hugging the shore, mingling with entrepreneurs looking for new opportunities, and "lateral thinkers" hoping to leverage every breath of wind for gain.

If Paul were traveling today, no doubt he would also imagine the body of Christ in movement by air, either business class or coach, sharing the news about the risen Jesus out there somewhere in the wild blue yonder in mission to fellow travelers, people waiting at the gate, fast-food providers, and anyone with a spare moment. He would imagine the body of Christ in movement by Internet, Web-based or free-running email, following AOL protocols to be brief, clear, and generous, and move on. By land or by sea, in real time or virtual time, the body of Christ is the road runner of the twenty-first-century pagan world.

The apostles shunned the fixed assets of property, polity, and prosperity in favor of portable spirituality. In addition to a sack of food, a change of clothes, and the tools of their trade, they carried what might be called the essentials of abundant life:

- *A transforming experience.* They all carried the bubbling excitement of an encounter with God incarnate, the experience of which had changed their lives positively and forever. They could recognize this incarnate God in many places and in many forms, but the experience was definitively revealed in Jesus.

- *A specific narrative.* They all carried a story, not always with quite the same chronology, and sometimes with different anecdotes, but nevertheless the same essential story about the birth, life, death, and resurrection of a unique person whose mere existence changed everything. It was a story in which this life, their lives, and the life of the world were inextricably bound together.

- *A peculiar companionship.* They all carried an open invitation to anyone (imperial messenger or runaway slave, male or female, Greek or Jew) to join a community united by a single, confident hope in the victory of good over evil. This community was not bound by ethnicity, family obligation, ritual practice, bodily scars, secret knowledge, or political power, but by a mutual love that would be as predictable at one end of the Empire as another.

- *An alternative lifestyle.* They all modeled a pattern of behavior that made ordinary people *better* than even the wealthy, empowered aristocrats. Their peace, patience, kindness, gentleness, joy, and self-control made them stand out among the tribes, sects, and conspiracies of the times. So odd and inoffensive did they seem that Pliny the Younger would write Emperor Trajan that their supposed guilt amounted to no more than this: "they had met regularly before dawn on a fixed day to chant verses . . . in honour of Christ . . . and also to bind themselves by oath . . . to abstain from theft, robbery, and adultery, to commit no breach of trust and not to deny a deposit when called upon to restore it.[3] After this ceremony it had been their custom to disperse and reassemble later to take food of an ordinary, harmless kind."[4]

- *An urgent mission.* They all acted like they had not a moment to lose, as if they needed to unburden themselves of momentous tidings, or as if they need to bring to closure important matters, which if neglected might break a sacred trust. Once their story had been told,

their invitation shared, their companionship con-
firmed, and their lifestyle rooted in a new location, they
became so restless for the open road that they could not
be held back for long.

This portable spirituality led them to adopt an unusual sign of
recognition for the open road. The fish symbol had nothing to do
with the Greek spelling of Jesus' name, and even less with memories of the unimportant Sea of Galilee few had seen. It simply
referred to the universal distinction of two different kinds of people. There are passive people and active people, people who
watch and people who act, people who talk about Jesus and people who follow Jesus. In a world where people either fish or cut
bait, Christians drew an image in the dust that revealed unequiv-
ocally their inclination: *I fish!* I do not cut bait. I do not just put a
denarius in the offering plate and watch the mission go by. I walk
the road looking for Jesus, way, way beyond Emmaus.

—Today's Pagan World —

The precarious situation of the church today results from a mis-
perception of the true state of the twenty-first-century world, and
a misunderstanding of the role Christianity plays in it. This is *not*
a Christian world, and although church leaders intellectually
acknowledge their diminished market share of contemporary culture, their actual behavior reveals that they grossly overestimate
their influence on culture and underestimate the influence of
pagan religion on the spiritualities of the public and their own
institutional religion. This is a pagan world similar to that of the
first century. The word *pagan* does not imply the dogmatic or ideological condescension toward contemporary culture that nine-
teenth-century Christian mission had toward those "poor,
wayward savages" yet to be blessed by European ways. The word
pagan is simply a description of the way things are. Our world is
akin to the first-century Roman Empire: culturally diverse, technologically innovative, militarily powerful, simultaneously

blessed for its peacekeeping and hated for its power. Leaders in that ancient world were sophisticated, talented, educated, and astute human beings. Just as it is today, people then of all social classes considered themselves deeply spiritual and morally responsible people, *but they were not Christians.*

I know what many readers are thinking. The claim that postmodern and premodern experiences are similar is not new, and the observation that today's religious and cultural diversity has undermined Christianity's religious dominance is not original. Many have railed against the corruption of Christianity as "civil religion," and have entirely missed the point. Twenty-first-century America is not *analogous* to the pagan culture of the first century. It *is* the pagan culture of the first century. The traditional modern church is not a distorted version of Christian community waiting to be purified, but, rather, is the legitimate, reasonable, established paganism that Paul, Silas, Lydia, Aquila, and the earliest road runners left behind in Jerusalem, challenged in Rome, and criticized in every port, way station, and town across the Mediterranean world. The "pagan" world is not a sociological background for ecclesiastics to condescendingly reflect on cultural and religious diversity, but, rather, an existential phenomenon in which real people desperately search for truth and the purpose of living while being pulled in a hundred directions at once.

The comparison of the twenty-first century to the first century is more literally accurate than church denominational leaders care to admit. Traditional modern churches (conservative or liberal) still expect the majority of church members to "cut bait" in the clouded belief that the need to "fish" is not particularly urgent. Indeed, as members simply attend worship services, maintain infrastructures, and send money to generic denominational operating funds, the denominations establish "fish processing plants" that make fine distinctions between the right kind of fish and the wrong kind of fish. They invent new ways to package fish, freeze fish, and even genetically engineer fish, but the prospect of actually *fishing* is somewhat loathsome and disreputable. Meanwhile, church educational institutions train leaders who teach church members how to "cut bait" extremely well. Today, when you see an automobile bumper sticker with the sign of the fish, it really proclaims *I am passionately committed to raise money to pay somebody else to fish!*

In Roman times, about 10 percent of the population across the Empire lived in cities, and 90 percent lived in the country. By the first century, wealth, power, education, health care, entertainment, and even guaranteed grain supplies had all shifted to an urbanized subculture. Meanwhile, the 90 percent living in the country rapidly lost control over their property and civil rights as absentee urban landlords displaced them with slaves who could make the land more profitable. This increased the number of people available for military service, encouraged migration to the cities, multiplied the number of poor prepared to sell themselves temporarily into servitude in a desperate attempt to improve their lives, and of course increased the number of discontented zealots. This explains why the early Christian movement shifted so rapidly from being a rural religion to being an urban religion. Christian road runners traveled the links between urban centers to share the welcome relief of Jesus among the people most receptive to experience it. So effective were they that by the second century, the Christian church had to strategize ways to reach out to the country dwellers *(paganus)*. That posed a problem. The now urbane Christian institution had to find ways to communicate with the larger population who were illiterate, superstitious, and trapped by economic forces beyond their control.

In North American times, a very similar situation has arisen. About 10 percent of the global village has the wealth, power, education, health care, leisure, and food, and about 90 percent of the people live beyond this urbanity with alternate learning methodologies and sundry beliefs, trapped by economic forces beyond their control. The line between the 10 percent and 90 percent may not be geographically as clear as the walls surrounding the Roman city, but they are just as real. In the Christendom centuries, the Christian movement not only infiltrated the subculture of the elite 10 percent, but it was itself transformed from a "movement" to an "institution." The road runners all became temple priests. Obsessed with sacred property and membership privileges, rationalized into dogmas and doctrines, organized into denominational polities, civilized by rules of order, preoccupied with Sunday as a "day of rest" and sports participation, and centered around fellowship and potluck suppers, church has become so entangled with the culture of the elite that in the twenty-first century it faces a problem. How does the now urbane Christian institution find ways to share the experience of Jesus with the *paganus* who make up most of the tribes and subcultures today? Indeed, does the church even *want* to do so?

It is really not hard to compare the first-century Roman world to the twenty-first-century North American world because it is the same world. In addition to the unprecedented opportunities to travel, the migration of people to the city, and the emergence of a new elite, consider the following:

- Both worlds rely on a form of "slavery" as the foundation of their economies. Slavery in the Roman Empire was not necessarily the brutal abuse modern people associate with the suppression of African people in the Deep South. It was simply a means by which individuals and whole families could ensure their livelihood and improve their lot in life. Americans in the penal system best resemble the minority of slaves in the Roman Empire who worked in the mines. The majority of Roman slaves were laborers, artisans, domestics, and professionals. They all worked under the control of an elite class. Some slaves became quite wealthy. Many professionals (doctors, teachers, and so forth) were freed. Many laborers and domestics preferred to remain in slavery because their quality of life was better.

  When people today speak of being "slaves to the company," "slaves to the office," or "slaves to the almighty dollar," they are not using metaphors. They are describing the same literal truth as the slaves of Rome. Some slaves will invest in the stock market and become wealthy. Many professional slaves will retire at age fifty-five and enjoy a good pension. Many middle management and laboring slaves will quit their jobs, but willingly indenture themselves to another boss.

• Both worlds maintain fairly rigid class boundaries in a pyramid of affluence and influence. In the Roman world, fewer than five hundred families held most of the wealth and power. The equestrian class (.01% of the population) and the decurion class (5%) held intermediate positions of authority. Only one tenth of the population was respectable Roman citizens with special exemptions from taxes, extra legal rights, and marriage legitimacy. In the first century, it was not easy to obtain "respectability," and extremely difficult to penetrate the upper classes. Wealth, status, and virtue were linked together.

Whatever the constitutional guarantees and promises in North America, the facts of life most closely resemble the Roman world. The pyramid remains in place. It is not just that wealth and influence go together, but that wealth and esteem go together. The wealthier one is, the better the health care becomes, the more accessible higher education becomes, the more legal sanctions offer protection, and the less the tax burden is. Many might object to this as an exaggeration. However, the fact remains that as the public becomes less upwardly mobile, lotteries multiply, speculation in stocks multiplies, and inquiring minds want to idolize the rich and famous, just like in the Roman Empire.

• Both worlds elevate leisure and sport as social necessities. The first-century Roman world may not have had weekends in the sense we do today, but Romans had as many or more official holidays as we do today. The popular Roman graffiti "Baths, wine and love-making destroy our bodies, yet love-making, wine and baths make life worth living" might easily be written today. The Roman bath as a popular meeting place for gossip is the ancient equivalent of today's mall food court. Alcohol and other drugs are as popular now as then. Sex and pornography are as commonplace today as in the ancient world.

First- and twenty-first-century people share a passion for spectacle and aggressive behavior. Huge amphitheaters are built in every town of any size now for football as they were then for gladiatorial combat. Games of all kinds attract huge crowds who idolize specific teams and athletes. Roman theater has been replaced by modern movies. The one hundred satellite television stations serve much the same purpose as the many Roman holidays, entertaining the masses and diverting them from the grinding routine of daily life.

Life and death in pagan Rome or pagan North America are alike. Dual-career families work very hard in difficult circumstances, spend most of their time away from their tiny tenement apartments, form alliances with some subcultures and bitterly resent others, lament the disobedience of teenagers, fear the dark, and spend too much money honoring the dead with meaningless rituals.

In a pagan world, the road runners bringing the welcome relief of Jesus Christ were both a blessing and a curse. On the one hand, the Christians empowered people to cross class boundaries, live a gentler and purer lifestyle, and hope for an end to slavery. On the other hand, after careful consideration, many people actually preferred to live in class boundaries, enjoyed violent and decadent lifestyles, and hoped to enslave other people in their need to control. It is not difficult to imagine why Christians in the old or new apostolic age are both welcomed and persecuted, perhaps even on the same day and by the same people.

Today's Pagan Spirituality

The modern traditional church functions in exactly the same way as Roman official religion did in the first century. Whether in magnificent temples or wayside shrines, great cathedrals or rural parishes, the church embodies the official religion of the land. The names of "Jesus," "Mary," "Matthew, Mark, Luke, and John," and other saints are reminiscent of the earlier Christian movement, but the behavior surrounding these names has become wooden, institutional, and stereotypical. In times of crisis (whether invasion by the Carthaginians or terrorist attacks on the World Trade Center), Romans and North Americans acted the same, by flocking to the centers of official religion to sacrifice to Jupiter or pray to God. This spiritual habit is certainly sincere and well intentioned, but the behavior pattern is distinctly pagan. The practice of religious faith and the welfare of the state go hand in hand.

The pagan world (past and present) merges civic duty and religion. Religion is a contract between the gods and humanity in which the egos of the gods are appeased by ritual behavior patterns performed by humans. Humans make requests of the gods for prosperity, health, fertility, peace, safe travel, legal justification, sports victory, and other matters, and the gods reward those who have been most dutiful in performing the rituals. The popular statements found in the personal ads in newspapers across North America thanking St. Jude or the Holy Spirit "for favors received" is pagan religion in its purest form.

In pagan religion you can believe whatever you like, so long as the traditional rituals are performed properly. Thus Roman pagans were so obsessed with ritual that they provided assistants to the priests who would repeat the same prayers several times to make sure that not a single syllable was forgotten or misspoken. Thus American pagans are so obsessed with ritual that quarrels over "good worship" or "good music" divide churches more often than any other issue (including doctrinal or ideological differences).

In pagan religion, there is always room for one more god. God and ethnicity are closely linked together, so as the pagan world encompasses more and more subcultures and personal perspectives, so also the identities of the gods are merged and blended in new ways. Here are comparative lists of the pantheon of the gods:

Greek	Roman	North American	God or Goddess of . . .
Zeus	Jupiter	"A Higher Power"	Sky, thunder, addiction relief
Hera	Juno	"The Goddess"	Women, sexuality, feminism
Athena	Minerva	"Higher Education"	Wisdom, crafts, scientific method
Apollo	Apollo	"The Media"	Youth, music, television, radio
Asclepius	Aesculapius	"American Medical Society"	Healing, wealth, the good life
Ares	Mars	"The United States Marines"	War, peacekeeping, heritage
Hestia	Vesta	"Bob Vila" or "Martha Stewart"	Hearth, roots, home renovation
Hermes	Mercury	"Hollywood"	Eloquence, thieves, entertainers
Demeter	Ceres	"Genetic Engineers"	Fertility, grain, DNA
Hephaestus	Vulcan	"Dow Jones"	Fire, industry, stock markets
Poseidon	Neptune	"Microsoft"	Sea, water, Internet
Aphrodite	Venus	"Sex"	Love, intimacy, romance novels
Artemis	Diana	"Mother Nature"	Woods, seasons, ecology
Tyche	Fortuna	"Las Vegas"	Luck, good fortune, lotteries
Dionysus	Bacchus	"Budweiser"	Wine, debauchery, good times

Many might think the above list is deliberately facetious, but it is not. True religious authority is revealed in the spontaneous habits of the public, the priorities they assign time and money, and the manner in which they observe birth, marriage, and death. When you look at habits, lifestyle priorities, and life cycle practices, you discover that the modern traditional church is simply a blending of various gods from multiple subcultures.

Pagan religion is remarkably tolerant of beliefs. Even so, we can observe how the official church (whether self-identified as conservative or liberal) is actually receptive to many different gods. Intolerance of other beliefs only emerges when it becomes a threat to civil authority or the customary way of life. Then the belief, whatever it is, is labeled "fanatical" or "cultic" and is proscribed by law or community mores. This periodically happened in the first century to the Christian road runners bringing the welcome relief of Jesus Christ to the public. It periodically happens in the twenty-first century to spiritual entrepreneurs starting or revitalizing congregations. Christian leaders in the first century might be thrown in prison or recalled to the central office in Jerusalem. Christian leaders in the twenty-first century might lose their tax-exempt status with the IRS or be recalled to the denominational office for contradicting polity or offending denominational "ethos."

In addition to official religion, the pagan world (ancient and contemporary) celebrates emperor worship. This was originally initiated by Caesar Augustus to strengthen his hold on the eastern provinces where rulers were traditionally deified since the time of the Persian Empire. The most troublesome provinces were governed directly by the emperor, and most Roman legions were stationed there. The emperor paid the administrators of the provinces and salaries of the soldiers from his personal funds. The cult of the emperor, therefore, was a useful vehicle to build morale and ensure the personal loyalty of those who enforced his authority.

In the western Roman Empire emperor worship became the cult of Roma, in which the "genius" or "inner spirit" of the empire embodied in the person of the emperor was worshiped. Vespasian was called "Lord" and his son Titus called "Savior." Worshipers would swear oaths to the nation incarnate in the emperor, and perhaps sacrifice a bull or burn incense. People could worship other gods as well, but they had to swear allegiance to *this* god in particular. Thus, for Christians and Jews it became a test to discover who was really loyal to the state.

It is this latter cult of emperor worship that figures most strongly in pagan North America. When the prime minister of Canada was assaulted with a pie thrown in his face, public outrage was disproportionate to the act itself. The nation incarnate in the person of the prime minister had been insulted. Similarly, the president of the United States represents a national identity that is worshiped in pagan America. Adoration of the flag, as well as movies or television programs like *The American President* and *The West Wing* popularize stereotypical and idealistic notions of country and office.

Occasionally an oath of national allegiance has been used as a test to differentiate between legitimate religions tolerated by the state, and fanaticism not tolerated by the state. Modern versions of the cult of Roma are not the property of the religious right, but run throughout North American culture and interface with all brands of the institutional church. In a sense, the controversy over prayer in public school or swearing oaths of allegiance in God's name is not a quarrel between atheists and theists, but between the cult of Roma and polytheism. In pagan North America as in pagan Rome, the genius of the nation ("The American Way," "O Canada, True North and Free") does not exclude other gods, but does demand allegiance above all gods.

The cult of Roma, in its eastern manifestation, has significantly diminished under the biting sarcasm of *Saturday Night Live* and David Letterman. Few equate the divine right of the state with the divinity of the prime minister or president (even though the heads of the gods from the time of Augustus Caesar to Abraham Lincoln are still stamped on coins, and loyal citizens still rename ancient cities and contemporary airports after political leaders). The cult of Roma, in its western manifestation, however, is so entrenched in culture and religion as to be unnoticed. One may not feel obliged to sacrifice a bull or eat turkey on Thanksgiving Day (although the issue has become increasingly stressful for Arab Americans and other minorities), but one must obtain a Social Security or Social Insurance number to participate in society.

Finally, the pagan world (ancient and contemporary) encourages a proliferation of mystery religions. Pagan Rome welcomed mystery religions related to Demeter, Orpheus, Isis, Cybele, and Mithras, among others.

- The myth of Demeter is manifest in North America as the mystery of "Mother Nature," often articulated among naturalists and environmentalists, or youth camping movements, or other back-to-nature sentiments.
- The myth of Orpheus supports the belief that human "souls" are trapped in the material world, and can be liberated at death or gradually freed through a series of reincarnations. One sees the mystery religion not only in the fascination with reincarnation, but in constant references, especially in funeral services, to "freed" or "perfected" souls that survive death.
- The myth of Isis focuses on human immortality or the divine spark that lies at the heart of humanity. Various forms of humanism glorify or idealize "man's humanity" as an enduring force through the ages.
- The myth of Cybele, the Earth Mother, surfaces in modern culture in various forms that may even be in conflict with one another. Sexuality, womanhood, or affirmative action for women may each use symbols of breast, womb, and procreation to represent the mysteries of life.
- The myth of Mithras describes the eternal war between good and evil, and focuses on the need for a militant mediator to rescue humanity. Various forms of dualism, the media preoccupation with Satan or vampires, or the idealization of the violent vigilante who rights wrongs are all part of popular paganism.

Pagan North America welcomes established world religions of all kinds, but almost always adapts them to serve purposes that indigenous followers do not intend. This is the syncretism or blending that is a hallmark of pagan life. Devotees flit from one mystery religion to another, often blending contradictory doctrines and reshaping images and symbols. Common elements in any mystery religion include:

- emphasis of the personal connection with the divine, and the personal salvation of the follower;
- fascination with birth and death, and major life cycle changes that are revelatory of eternal truth;
- preoccupation with life after death, or alternate existences alongside present reality;
- secret knowledge that explains gratuitous evil or guides to hidden meaning;
- secret rites that initiate a trusted few into a righteous community that can judge others.

Mystery "religions" do not need to be systematic, logical, or institutional, and in this sense they are not "religions" at all. They are patterns of superstition, behavior, or relationship to which people turn in times of crisis or confusion.

Official religion, the cult of Roma, mystery cults, and the multitude of personal spiritualities, all coexisted in the Roman world within a larger philosophical environment shaped by the educational institutions of the time. Philosophy and lifestyle merged. Epicureans, for example, cultivated lifestyles around taste and perceptions of beauty, just as North American subcultures build lifestyles around music, fashion, food, or home decorating. These lifestyles can be articulately defended and interpreted to give meaning to life. Even cynicism could be established as a lifestyle and philosophy in itself. In contemporary North America, to be skeptical of everything is as much a philosophy (and can make as distinctive a fashion statement) as any particular belief or habit.

The dominant philosophy of the pagan upper class is a form of stoicism. The Stoics were among the best educated, most reasonable, and most humane leaders of their time. They particularly prized rational intellect, scientific deduction, inward integrity, clarity of purpose, and a keen sense of justice. The emperor Marcus Aurelius himself was a Stoic. Stoics valued close friendship, marriage and family loyalty, civic duty, and social justice. They tended to avoid extremes of materialism or extremes of consumption. They trained body, mind, and soul holistically. They were capable of extraordinary self-discipline and personal sacrifice. They could manage a business, lead an army, stick to a diet plan, and model the seven habits of successful living.

Today's stoics usually go to church regularly, and are frequently on governing boards of official religions. They are rigorous about ritual and passionate about heritage because such things maintain the purity of faith and preserve the welfare of the state. Stoics are comfortable with the cult of Roma and the destiny of the state, but very suspicious of emperor worship in itself and any aggrandizement of public office. They may even join or support a mystery religion or three because "all truth is one."

Official Christianity, like the official religion of Rome, exists as a kind of ritual expression of a larger philosophy of "the good life," and it coexists alongside other religions in the very attitudes and lifestyles of the church members. However, the more broadly scientific methodology is accepted to interpret reality, and the more passionately national identity is used to shape the goals of people, and the more powerfully mystery religions of all kinds address the longings of seekers, the less important official religion becomes to the people! In the first century, the ancient Romans were already lamenting the decline in offerings to support the traditional shrines, the decline in volunteers to serve as temple priests, and the decline in respect the masses gave to ancestral religion.

Enter the Christian road runners of the first and contemporary apostolic age. They share a transformational experience, tell a powerful story, celebrate an extraordinary companionship, model a meaningful alternative way of life, and inspire a sense of personal worth and destiny in Christ. Along the way they shift fundamental life metaphors away from ethnic identity to unity with the True Vine in the global vineyard, away from patriarchal Roman family to equality in "the body of Christ," and away from immobile social class to allegiance to a classless kingdom of God. People start behaving differently. Lives are transformed. The link between religion and state is severed, and the accepted norm of faith in many gods is replaced by allegiance to one God perfectly revealed in a crucified man.

These early Christians are twice rejected. They are rejected by the pagan public for being atheists. They deny the existence of the gods and the right of individuals to choose whatever god fulfills their personal needs. The public thinks Christians are narrow-minded bigots. They are also rejected by their own kind for being fanatics. They deny the institutional foundations of Christian denominationalism and the liberal sentiment that in the end "we all believe the same thing." Caught between accusations that they do not believe anything at all, and accusations that they believe one thing too much, Christian road runners become endangered in the pagan world.

The Roman Suetonius expresses the perspective of learned, spiritual, twenty-first-century professionals when he describes this Christianity as "a novel and mischievous superstition" (*Vita Neronis* 16).[5] In a pagan world, the problem with real Christianity is not that it is dogmatically pure or ideologically correct, but that it is simply disreputable. No intelligent, self-respecting, truly spiritual person should avail himself of it.

Nevertheless, public interest in the Christian movement grows and grows. Credibility for the official religion of the institutional church will continue to decline as it did in the first century. Confidence in the manifest destiny of the state will continue to erode as it did in the first century. Fulfillment through personal mystery religions will continue to disappoint as it did in the first century. The resulting vacuum of authentic spirituality and deep longing for a real hope will create openness to the welcome relief of Jesus Christ as never before. Christian road runners, the mavericks of the institutional church, will become the most valuable leaders of a revitalized Christian movement.

Notes

1. James S. Jeffers, *The Greco-Roman World of the New Testament Era* (Downers Grove, Ill.: InterVarsity Press, 1999), pp. 34-35.

2. Ronald Hock, *The Social Context of Paul's Ministry: Tentmaking and Apostleship* (Philadelphia: Fortress Press, 1980), p. 27.

3. W. W. Meissner, *The Cultic Origins of Christianity* (Collegeville, Minn.: Liturgical Press, 2000), pp. 152-59.

4. Betty Radice, trans. *The Letters of the Younger Pliny* 10.96 (Baltimore: Penguin, 1963), p. 294.

5. Jeffers, *The Greco-Roman World of the New Testament*, p. 22.

Two

THE BODY IN MOTION

The constant traveling done by the apostles and missionaries in the earliest church is essential to the identity of the Christian community. It is not just that the leaders were itinerant preachers, or that the selected missionaries were sent to distant mission fields, but that the entire body of Christ was in constant, dynamic motion. The members of the body might have various spiritual gifts, in fulfillment of which they might perform in certain ways (Eph. 4:1-16). Each member of the body might have his or her uniqueness, which contribute to the overall unity of the body (1 Cor. 12:12-31). What was unspoken, because it seemed so obvious to the earliest Christians, was that this "body" should be in *motion*. Everybody was a traveler. Every member was in process. The eye cannot say to the hand, "I have no need of you," and the hand cannot say to the foot, "You go on, and I'll stay behind to do the fund-raising." Every part of the body goes, or no part of the body goes. Luke's motivation for writing the Acts of the Apostles was his conviction that God's message to Philip (Acts 8:26-40) reveals the essential identity of the church: *Get up and go!* No sooner has Philip been spirited away to the Gaza road where he baptizes the Ethiopian traveler in a mud puddle, than

Sermon · "Immediately on the way" — Comma dist ath, on the way

he is again spirited away to the Gentile cities of Azotus and Caesarea.

The earliest church never conceived itself an institution. That is why they felt no particular competition with the synagogue or established religions in other parts of the empire. They considered themselves a *movement*. There was a restlessness, a pragmatism, and a remarkable resistance in the earliest church to be tied down to any particular place, organizational structure, or set of religious rites. It is said that the New Testament can be used to justify almost any organizational structure from episcopacy to utopian community, but modern traditional church people always miss the real point. Christendom wants to freeze the movement into a structure. Christendom believes that there is an *inevitability* about structure, stasis, immobility, and rest. The difference between the earliest church and later Christendom is that the latter believes movement is a temporary transition between rest stops, and the earliest Christians believed rest was a temporary hiatus from traveling, taken just to catch your breath.

Two forces precipitate the body of Christ into motion. Both are perceived as the work of the Spirit, although one is experienced painfully and the other joyfully.

First, rejection by the world precipitates movement. This rejection may be in the form of violent persecution. The Sanhedrin and Pharisees attacked the fledgling church (Acts 6–8), and the apostles fled from Jerusalem to be scattered abroad. Paul, Timothy, Silas, and company are repeatedly assaulted, arrested, or persecuted by agitators from the synagogue, devotees of other cults, and civil authorities. Rejection may not be violent, however. Hearts may just not be open. Communities may simply be indifferent. Class-consciousness may be insurmountable. The body of Christ moves on. There is a growing awareness of being "in the world" but not "of the world." The early church leaders warn: "Do not be astonished, brothers and sisters, that the world hates you" (1 John 3:13). Such a sense of rejection could result in paranoia, and drive the body of Christ into flight or defensiveness, were it not for the other precipitating factor of the spirit.

This second factor, passionate love for the world, precipitates movement. Modern people want this love to be agapic—self-sacrificial, altruistic, charitable—because it makes better sense to an institution at rest. Yet there are few charitable "programs" mentioned in the earliest church, only expectations incumbent on every member for spiritual life. There is little self-deprecation among the apostles, but rather a confidence and aggressiveness often offensive to modern people. Eros, not *agape,* is the passionate love that precipitates movement. It is the desire for fulfillment of one's destiny with Jesus, the desire to be with Christ.

> Yet whatever gains I had, these I have come to regard as loss . . . because of the surpassing value of knowing Christ Jesus my Lord. For his sake I have suffered the loss of all things, and I regard them as rubbish, in order that I may gain Christ and be found in him." (Phil. 3:7-9*a*)

Paul's words express the Eros that impels his movement. He desires to be with Jesus. If Jesus is in the mission field, Paul is in the mission field. If Jesus is going to Rome, Paul is going to Rome. If Jesus suffers, Paul will suffer. If Jesus has come down from the cross, Paul will come down from the cross. The Greek word translated as "rubbish" is a coarse and powerful word. Paul treats all of his advantages of birth, education, and privilege as *shit* because of the surpassing joy of being with Jesus.

The cult film *The Matrix* has been hailed as revealing the great shift in perception from the modern to the postmodern world. That shift is the recognition that the seeming solidity, continuity, reliability, or structure of reality is, in fact, a large-scale hallucination, and that in truth reality is an experience of constant fluidity, change, and motion. Whether or not you embrace the Christian symbolism of the movie, you sense the radically different perception of reality shared by Paul, Lydia, and the earliest church in premodern times. The monolithic stability of the Roman world is, to them, a mass hallucination. The monuments and cities and aqueducts, even the finely engineered Roman roads on which they travel, are unreal. The Pax Romana is a peace that is unreal.

The religious rites, rules of law, circumcision of the body, temple sacrifices, ordained priesthood, wondrous sculpture on the Acropolis of Athens are unreal. The seeming stability and structure are unreal. What is real is the fluidity of spirit, the movement of God, the sweeping process of salvation, in which every person is swept away. The body of Christ, therefore, is in motion, just as the spirit is in motion, and to freeze the body in any way (yesterday or tomorrow) is to acquiesce to the essential unreality of the mass hallucination of Christendom.

Those familiar with the plot of *The Matrix* will recall the turning point of faith in the lead character called Neo. The mentor, Morpheus, says to him: "Neo, sooner or later you need to realize, just as I did, that there is a difference between knowing the path and walking the path." This insight marks the great divide from the premodern world of the ancient church, to the modern world of Christendom, and back again to the postmodern world of the twenty-first century.

- It the difference between explaining the Nicene Creed, and refusing to burn incense to the cult of Roma;
- It is the difference between knowing the Bible, and working for the restoration of Eden;
- It is the difference between surrendering your life to Christ, and surrendering your lifestyle to Jesus.

I have been coaching congregations and faith-based organizations in the discernment of "genetic code" (the core identity of values, beliefs, vision, and mission that is embedded in every cellular unit, member, and leader of an organism) for years. The single, continuing obstacle is that modern people persist in thinking a core value to be an agreement about public policy, a bedrock belief to be an abstract principle, a vision to be a statement, and a mission to be survival. These are modern addictions, based on the mass hallucination that the real world is a stable, predictable structure that can be encompassed by corporate policy, rationalization, articulate learning, and predictability. In the *real* world of the earliest church—the world of fluidity and spirit—these things did not shape identity.

- Behavior patterns replace public policy as the source of core values;
- Symbols replace principles as the source of bedrock beliefs;
- Stories replace statements as the source of vision;
- Growth replaces survival as the source of mission.

The body of Christ is not shaped by public policy, elaborate creeds, wishful thinking about the future, or preservation of heritage. That is the body at rest. That is the body compromised by the unreal world. The body of Christ for Paul, Lydia, ancient and postmodern Christians, is the body *in motion.* It is shaped by positive, predictable behavior patterns ("fruits of the Spirit" [Gal. 5:22]), by symbols of faith (graffiti hastily scribbled as catacomb art while listening for the soldiers at the door), by transformational stories of hope (resurrection narratives), and by constant holistic growth ("growing up into Christ" [see Eph. 4:15]).

The Gnostic Competition

This shift from "knowing the path" to "walking the path" has a deeper significance in both the ancient and postmodern world— a significance that greatly affects our understanding of the church. The greatest threat to Christianity in the early years was not from persecution by other religions or cults. Indeed, the greatest threat was not even from the cult of Roma. Sporadic persecutions caused some Christians to die in the arena. There is some evidence that Nero scapegoated Christians in Rome for the devastating fire he himself probably caused. There is also evidence that even the Roman pagans pitied the Christians for the injustice they experienced. The real threat to early Christianity came from Gnosticism; and the real threat to postmodern Christianity also comes from Gnosticism.

Gnosticism was not a religion, but an amorphous spirituality that pervaded the latter part of the first century, peaked in the second century, and all but disappeared by the third century. We know of its pervasiveness and persuasiveness through a few surviving manuscripts, and by the attacks made upon it by Christian leaders. The aggressiveness of Christian critique gives evidence to the power of its influence. Gnosticism reemerges in history among Mandeans in Iraq, Bogomils in Bulgaria, and Catharists (Albigensians) in medieval France, but it would be a mistake to associate this broad worldview with any locality or time. It is the most powerful threat to the body of Christ today.

Gnosticism is a spirituality that emphasizes special knowledge of divine mysteries: an exclusive or privileged insight into the workings of the universe, the destiny of humankind, the origins of good and evil, or the nature of God. It is at once technical and mystical. The true Gnostic smiles benevolently on the spiritual inquirer and says, "Ah, my son, this is far too complicated for you to understand." Or the true Gnostic rebukes criticism and says, "You fool, this is deeper and more profound than your limited sensibilities could ever comprehend." Before considering the content of Gnostic spirituality, notice the methodology of Gnostic practice, because in many ways the methodology is what is most appealing to modern people.

- *It is a "special knowledge."* This "knowledge" may be complicated or hidden, but it is still a rational databank that can be probed, examined, and understood by the mind. Gnosticism then and now appeals to the well educated; to people with a deep-seated conviction that knowledge leads to power. In an industrial society, it is influential. In an information society, it is extraordinarily powerful. Teachers, academics, engineers, corporate executives, and professionals of all kinds love it. It treats religion like a more complicated astrophysics, history like an intricate social analysis, and the human soul as a level of aesthetic sophistication. "If only you knew the right language, possessed the right analytical tools, associated with the right people, and appreciated the right music, the divine spark within you just might be saved!"

- *It is a special knowledge known by an elite few.* This "knowledge" is the intellectual property of a limited number of people. Depending on the brand of Gnosticism, the elite may be identified by their educational credentials, by their militant attitudes, by their priestly robes, or by self-flagellation. They may have a large following, but the secrets of life, death, God, and the future are reserved for an inner circle who are deemed worthy. "If only you shared the right ideology, affirmed the right dogma, joined the right denomination, participated in the right microculture, you might have access to the real truth!"

To this extent the movie *The Matrix* is a product of Gnostic sensitivity. The "secret knowledge" about reality is known only by a select few who are initiated into the inner circle by swallowing a red pill. The knowledge requires advanced computer technology, and the discovery that hidden behind the appearance of the real world is the mind control of a world of machines. All of ignorant humanity goes about its daily business, but the few who possess the secret knowledge have absolute freedom.

Among all the possible variations, Gnosticism yesterday and today has three basic themes[1]:

1. *Alienation from the physical world that devalues the environment.* People not only reject the importance of the physical world, but resent the imprisonment of their inner–divine spark by bodies that age, become diseased, and die. Rampant materialism and environmental indifference thrives side by side with arrogant glorifications of self and the destiny of humanity.
2. *Obsession with the origin and significance of evil.* People fill the void between absolute nostalgia for the good and the total dread of pain with hundreds of supernat-

ural powers of varying strength ("demi-urges") on which bad experiences can be blamed. Rigid asceticism and interpersonal manipulation become twin avenues of control through which the individual can overcome obstacles and liberate the divine spark within.

3. *Desire for exclusive knowledge of the secrets of the universe.* People interpret history, conduct scientific research, and indulge lifestyle experiments confident that there is a secret set of facts, calculations, or behavior patterns that will explain every conundrum and resolve every ethical ambiguity. Technological sophistication and mystical speculation combine to promise a power to control the universe as yet unknown in daily life.

It is not hard to trace Gnostic beliefs and practices in contemporary life, science, art, and the media. As I write these words, thousands of people are driving environmentally unfriendly SUVs to the theater, burdened with questions about good and evil, in order to watch hit movies like *Harry Potter and the Sorcerer's Stone* and *The Lord of the Rings.* They identify themselves as Presbyterian, Baptist, or Mennonite in the national census. May the force be with them!

Gnostic influence (ancient and contemporary) generates an aura of profundity, but is remarkably unproductive. After all, the material world is of no consequence, so why bother to change it? Use it and enjoy it. Only a chosen few can penetrate the secret knowledge, so why try to convince anyone to behave differently? Use them and enjoy them. Gnostic spirituality is suggestive of insight of universal import, and yet is remarkably vague about details. The upshot of it all is that somehow, someday, I myself will be OK.

To sum up the essential position of the Gnostics in still simpler terms, let us say that in their eyes the evil which taints the whole of creation and alienates man in body, mind, and soul, deprives him of the awareness necessary for his own salvation.

Man . . . possesses only a shadow of consciousness . . . Gnostics . . . devoted themselves . . . to create in man a true consciousness, which would permit him to impart to his thoughts and deeds the permanence and the rigour necessary to cast off the shackles of this world.[2]

Once the hidden spark of divinity is uncovered, the human being can transcend this world to unite with God.

The impact of Gnostic spirituality on early Christian faith directly undermined the message of the apostolic road runners. They came equipped with a transforming experience, a resurrection narrative, an inclusive companionship, a peaceable lifestyle, and an urgent desire to give life away to others. Gnostics received the good news of a different way of life and hope for eternity, and made of it a methodology for privileged position in this world and the next. The same twisting of the gospel from universal hope to personal privilege is happening in the modern traditional church.

- The salvation history disclosed in the Old Testament and early Christian stories was discounted or mocked because the players in that history were ignorant of the real secrets of the universe. They were limited by their cultural context, confused about politically correct ideology, and biased in their perspective. The narrative of the road runner became more personal prejudice than welcome relief.
- The inclusive companionship that overcame class consciousness was outwardly praised and inwardly ridiculed, because only an elite could really know the truth. The cross-cultural sensitivity of the road runner became "dumbing down the gospel."
- The peaceable lifestyle that modeled the fruits of the spirit was mocked as impractical or denounced as insufficient. It either couldn't be done in a modern world, or didn't go far enough to radicalize public policy. The integrity of the road runner was cast as bigotry toward other religions.

- The transformational experience with Christ was disengaged from the historical life of Jesus. Christ could never be defiled by a physical body, and his supposed "death" could have no saving significance. Salvation was something a few people achieved, not a gift available to all people.

Gnosticism poses a threat to the Christian movement because it brings the body of Christ to a dead stop. Instead of traveling the countryside sharing welcome relief to oppressed people, it is rendered inert to gaze at the stars and initiate the elect into secret knowledge.

Modern traditional churches are possessed of a more moderate version of Gnosticism. It avoids the extremes of asceticism and mysticism. These Gnostics are among the most professional, most socially responsible people in the community. They eat fast food, but promote physical fitness. They extend their credit, but believe in fiscal responsibility. They believe the church is a good institution, but are convinced you can be a good Christian (perhaps a better Christian) without it. Christianity is a step along the path of spirituality from which really earnest or insightful people can graduate, usually at the age of maturity.

Today's Gnostics may or may not go to church regularly or at all, but if they are in church they militantly agitate for either pure spirituality or consistent ritual practice, but never both at the same time. Spirit and matter just don't go together. The sacrament can be celebrated any way at all, because the meaning has nothing whatever to do with the physical elements; or the sacrament must be celebrated precisely only one way, because the magic will only work if you do it right. Gnostics believe in either the divinity or humanity of Jesus, but never both together. They either make elaborate excuses to explain why the cross even matters to the essential "Jesus," or they spin passionate arguments about how the cross is an archetypal symbol of how the hidden God releases the divine spark within every human being. Never before has so much cappuccino been consumed while debating so esoteric a point.

Gnosticism seems to thrive best in the twilight of systemic change. At the high-water mark of a culture, it is embraced by the learned upper classes as a means of preserving their privileged status. They alone understand the nuances of theology. They alone practice the pure rites of liturgy. They alone keep the true spark of divinity alive. They invite the wider public to join them, but they are remarkably selective about who is initiated into the board of trustees, the ordained priesthood, or the policy governance of the denomination. On the other hand, Gnosticism seems to comfort the elite as the high tide of culture begins to recede. When the political expectations are not met, the just society is not achieved, the dogmatic consensus is not ratified, and the religions of the world do not settle down to enjoy a single potluck supper, then Gnosticism takes on an apocalyptic and mystical tone. Nostalgia for the past is replaced by nostalgia for the future, although it remains a rather vague nostalgia. Their day will come. Their cause will one day be vindicated. Their justification lies beyond the understanding of this world.

In this sense, Gnosticism is a not unexpected child of ancient Rome or modern North America. These people—well educated, idealistic, professional, technologically advanced, militarily potent, nationally proud—are convinced that there must be a data bank, a hidden knowledge, somewhere that will answer life's deepest questions and guarantee personal success. Structure, human intellect, and personal achievements represent the "reality" of the Roman and modern experience. Just as the ancients believed Hadrian's Wall would keep out the Picts, and the city of Rome would stand forever, so the eternal and immovable principles hidden before creation and available to a select few will stand firm against the tides of change. Technologies may change, but data banks are forever.

The Christian "Way"

Sooner or later you realize that there is a difference between "knowing" the path and "walking" the path. That is the difference modeled by the road runners of the earliest church, and articulated by Christian apologists for the first three centuries after Christ. It is the difference modeled by the road runners of the postmodern church, and articulated by Christian apologists for the next few centuries ahead.

Metaphors of "walking," "path," and "way" abound in the Old and New Testaments. Such metaphors clearly signify a way of life, or lifestyle, shaped by particular behavior patterns and attitudes, and guided by particular goals and obligations. It is never a matter of secret knowledge possessed only by an elite. God said to Abraham:

> "I am God Almighty; walk before me, and be blameless. And I will make my covenant between me and you, and will make you exceedingly numerous." (Gen. 17:1a-2)

Could anyone imagine that what is implied here is a secret knowledge or mystical data bank imparted exclusively to Abraham and passed on selectively to a handful of elite Israelites? In fact, Gnostic Jews inventing the mystical Kabbalah did just that through the third century, causing significant conflict within the synagogue. Jewish and Christian communities recognized the threat and opposed these Gnostic Jews. It's a *walk,* not a *knowledge.*

The New Testament describes Christianity specifically as the "Way" in three places. In each case, the Way is defined in opposition to an elitist special knowledge.

- Paul identifies himself as an original persecutor of the Way, because he believed he possessed an exclusive knowledge of salvation that allowed him to "know what was best" for others (see Acts 9:2 and 22:4).
- Ephesian community leaders loyal to the cult of Artemis attacked the Way because their mystery religion held that elite priests had special knowledge of the universe and observed rites that no ignorant human could understand (see Acts 19:9, 23).
- The Roman governor Felix had some familiarity with the Way, and understood why Paul distinguished it

from the knowledge-based sects spawned by other religions (Acts 24:14, 22).

The Way is not contrasted with other "ways," but rather with Gnostic spiritualities and other religions based on secret knowledge and an elite who are "in the know."

Modern commentators misunderstand the reference to the Way. They think the Way refers simply to a code of conduct, liturgical practice, and organizational polity. In other words, they think that the Way is simply another word for a "religion." This leads modern traditional Christians to worry excessively about Christianity making universal claims that might judge other religions. Yet the earliest road runners went to extremes to distinguish the Way from a religion. It was not a body of knowledge, a special diet plan, a universal liturgy franchised into every cultural corner, or an organizational structure. It was a Way—a fluid, dynamic, ever-changing, ever-fresh movement of spirit that always seemed to sidestep structures and resist rest.

The Way is best understood as the internalization of Jesus' own journey from birth to death to resurrection. This internalization of Jesus' journey to become *my* journey led the earliest road runners to turn their backs on society as they knew it, and strike out into the unknown on paths of extraordinary danger and personal fulfillment.

Internalization

Followers of the Way combined vivid imagination and physical activity to literally reenact the life, death, and new life of Jesus. At the close of the fourth century, Paulinus of Nola would write:

> "No other sentiment draws men [and women; there were actually more women pilgrims than men!] to Jerusalem than the desire to see and touch the places where Christ was physically present, and to be able to say from our very own experience 'we have gone into his tabernacle and adored in the very places where his feet have stood.' . . . Theirs is a truly spiritual desire to see the places where Christ suffered, rose from the dead, and ascended into heaven . . . all these things recall God's former

presence on earth and demonstrate the ancient basis of our . . . beliefs."[3]

This reference to pilgrimage to Jerusalem helps explain the internalization of Jesus' life experience in the heart of all the early road runners. Their whole life was a kind of "reenactment" of the life of Christ. They would read aloud the scriptures, recite the stories, place themselves in similar circumstances, and recall what Jesus said and did. This passion to be with Jesus, to live as he lived, and walk where he walked, lies at the core of the Way. Saint Jerome describes the emotions of his own protégé Paula when she visited the "holy places" for the first time:

> "She threw herself down in adoration before the cross as if she could see the Lord himself hanging from it. And when she entered the tomb, she kissed the stone which the angel had rolled away. . . . What tears she shed there, what sighs of grief . . . and when she looked upon the inn, the stall, and the crib . . . she cried out in my hearing that with the eyes of her soul she could see the infant Christ wrapped in swaddling clothes and crying in the manger."[4]

This desire to see "with the eyes of the soul," and to experience what Jesus experienced, is the core of the road runner. It is what participating in the Way means. That is what is implied by Paul's admonition "we walk by faith, not by sight" (2 Cor. 5:7), and again in Colossians 2:6: "As you therefore have received Christ Jesus the Lord, continue to walk in him" (see NRSV footnote). Paul desires to know Christ, sharing in his sufferings, walking with him on the road far, far beyond Emmaus, so that he can participate in his resurrection (see Phil. 3:10).

Contempt for the World

Followers of the Way engaged in a process of self-exile from the social, economic, and political realities of their day. It is not surprising that early road runners and later pilgrims would identify themselves more with the monastery than the parish church. The parish church had a sense of permanency, while the monastery was experienced as a way station isolated from the world. In the pilgrimage of the medieval world, the parish church charged pilgrims a fee to stay overnight, and the monasteries let them in free.

This contempt for the world could lead to excess. Some road runners became bandits, exercising their rejection of the world through violent attacks on villages and travelers, and some road runners might run into the desert seeking total isolation from humankind. The perversions are lamentable, but renouncing "the world" remains a key to the Way. The ancient hagiographer Heiric marveled to Charles the Bald:

> "Why is it that almost the entire population of Ireland, contemptuous of the perils of the sea, has migrated to our shores with a great crowd of teachers? The more learned they are the more distant their chosen place of exile."[5]

This is the other side of the maverick Christian leaders critical of, or rejecting totally, the modern traditional denominational systems. All the pension plans, medical benefits, and membership privileges seem to them to be "worldly." They would rather sail dangerous waters *with* Jesus than serve a parish church in the wealthiest port on earth.

The process of internalization leaves the road runner without any clear, physical destination. They have no clear goal to reside in a particular place, climb a particular career path, or retire to an economic standard. In this sense, they are true wanderers. They are as apt to change their course on a prayer, a whim, a sudden urge, or an unexpected calling, as Paul changed his destinations because somehow the "spirit" prohibited the team from going one place and opened a door of opportunity in another.

The process of contempt for the world leaves the road runner without any clear, physical point of origin. Ask them where they come from, and they can hardly find an answer. For Paul to say he is "from Tarsus" seems so irrelevant as to be hardly worth mentioning. They do not have a local accent to their speech. They do not wear clothes reminiscent of their heritage. They cannot even remember, much less quote, the polity under which they might have been ordained.

Road runners are truly "on the way." They neither look backward nor forward to define themselves. They are what they are, in company with Jesus, reenacting the life, death, and new life of Jesus every step of the way on the road to Emmaus and beyond.

Four Preparations to Be a Pilgrim

Modern traditional Christians balk at pilgrimage. This is as true for entire congregations as it is for individuals. They resist running on the open road. What will be the consequences? What is the strategic plan? What are the guarantees? What will become of the people left behind? What assurances are there of getting home safely? In 1406 a London preacher by the name of Richard Alkerton answered very simply:

> "He that be a pilgrim [bear in mind, of course, that a large percentage of pilgrims in ancient and medieval times were women] oweth first to pay his debts, afterwards to set his house in governance, and afterwards to array himself and take leave of his neighbours, and so go forth."[6]

Preparations in 1406 were really not much different from those of Philip in Acts 8, in which story God says "get up and go" and Philip got up and went. No strategic plan. No elaborate guarantees. Just do it.

In the comments that follow, be sure to understand that I am speaking as much about *congregations* as the "body of Christ," as I am about individual Christians. The temptation that has beset the church from the very beginning, and to which the modern traditional church has succumbed, is to apply behavioral expectation of pilgrimage on selected individuals, rather than to the "body of Christ" itself. By the later Middle Ages, wealthy community leaders were paying professional proxies to go crusade in their place, and affluent Christian congregations were paying professional

proxies to go on pilgrimage in their place! It was easier to pay
someone to do it for you (and receive an indulgence to forgive
one's sins), than to actually undertake the dangerous journey yourself. Today, modern traditional churches pay the clergy to "take
the cross" as a proxy for themselves (and receive an indulgence
every Sunday in the liturgical assurance of pardon), rather than
undertake to follow Jesus on the road to Emmaus themselves.

The general practice in early medieval times was to first make a
will. This was prudent, because it is estimated that 50 percent of
the pilgrims who set out never returned. Many died on the journey, were murdered, became lost, permanently relocated to Sinai,
or were still walking. Since most people care about their families
in the same way now as they did then, they make provisions for
them before hitting the open road. Second, a person should divest
himself of things. Not only can you not take many possessions
with you, but also the protection and transportation of too many
"things" will distract your imagination from pondering the companionship of Jesus. Third, a person should make amends with
his enemies. This is sound biblical advice. You not only avoid
having your enemies attack your friends and ransack your home-
stead in your absence, but also you walk with a clear conscience
and in harmony with your fellow travelers. Finally, pay your
debts. Eliminate the mortgage, cancel the lease on the Buick, and
stop running up the debt on your credit cards. No obligation will
hold you back, and no litigation will take you off the road.

The body of Christ itself makes a will, divests itself of "things,"
makes amends with its enemies, and pays its debts. It is not hard
to apply this lesson literally. Make sure your "dependents" are well
cared for (the poor, the lonely, the persecuted, the sick in your
community); get rid of old hymnbooks, chancel hardwood, and
useless stained glass that is too cumbersome or fragile for travel;
reconcile with neighboring churches, feuding factions, and the
IRS; give away the certified deposits and pay off the capital debt.
This advice can also be applied metaphorically. The body of
Christ bequeaths its wealth to the needy, turns its back on world-
liness, stops ranting about public policy and the distortions of the
media, and acknowledges its hidden obligations to the saints

(those under the age of eighteen and over seventy) and the two-thirds world.

For the modern traditional church, living in the security of perceived structures, polities, rational formulations, and databanks of knowledge (secular, sacred, or esoteric), the replies Jesus made to eager followers are unsettling. As I write this, I am traveling in Massachusetts where there is a city with two Anglo congregations struggling to survive unchanged in a community where 80 percent of the high school graduates speak Spanish. Will these churches choose to preserve their temples, wait for the demographics to "stabilize," and perhaps reassure themselves with esoteric knowledge discerned by their elite community about the end of the world? Or will they choose to follow Jesus into the mission field way beyond Emmaus?

- An unknown scribe declares that he will follow Jesus wherever he goes. Jesus replies: "Las zorras tienen guaridas, y las aves del cielo, nidos; pero el Hijo del hombre no tiene donde recostar su cabeza" (Mateo 8:20 Versión Reina-Valera, 1995). Jesus is on the move, and those who run the roads with him have neither an origin nor a destination to which they might return or to which they hope to retire. They let it all go to be with Jesus on the Way.
- Another would-be disciple declares his eagerness to go, but first asks permission to bury his deceased parent. Jesus replies: "Sígueme; deja que los muertos entierren a sus muertos" (Mateo 8:22 Versión Reina-Valera, 1995). Jesus is on the move, and those who share his mission urgency cannot be sidetracked by the perpetual maintenance of a cemetery with an endowment fund or memorials to family ancestors. They let it all go to be with Jesus on the Way.

This is the radical preparation required of postmodern Christians who want to walk with Jesus on the road to mission. In order to do it, they must let go various levels of modern sensibility. Most obviously, they must let go of the "things" that tempt them to remain at rest. More challenging yet, they must let go of a sense of duty to memorialize the past. Still more challenging, they must let go of the hidden presupposition that the world itself is an essentially static, structured reality that could be fully understood if only they could obtain "real knowledge" from the right consultant. Most challenging of all, they must let go the hidden elitism that somehow they "deserve" all that they have and that they know better than others what is good for the public. How hard it is for modern traditional Gnostics to walk the Way with Christ! They complain that the scriptures I quoted above have not been provided in the English language that most high school graduates in their community cannot understand, but which *they* read perfectly well.

Ten Habits of Healthy Road Runners

Once you have prepared yourself by making a will, divesting your material things, making peace with enemies, and paying your debts, the road runner sets out. Notice that the road runner has not memorized a strategic plan, and especially notice that the road runner does not carry in his or her head tomes of theological interpretation and gigabytes of esoteric knowledge. Instead, the road runner will:

1) Take the cross.
Just as Jerusalem pilgrims would carry heavy wooden crosses during Lent to share the sufferings of Christ, so also Christian road runners imagined they walked with the resurrected Jesus in joy and in sorrow on roads way, way beyond Emmaus. Modern people imagine pilgrims and crusaders adorning clothes and shields with tidy red crosses. In fact, they tattooed their bodies, and burned crude crosses into their flesh with a torch from the campfire. Talk about "embedding a vision"!
It is the incarnational core of the gospel that is essential. It is the confidence in Jesus Christ, fully human and fully divine, ulti-

mate mystery, scandal to the Gnostics, and cornerstone of abundant life that lies at the heart of road running. No ideological cause or theological principle, and no miraculous or supernatural destination, can motivate such movement. It is the relationship with Christ that is sufficient.

2. *Carry a staff.*

Aside from the cross, the large, tall, crude walking staff is the chief symbol of the road runner. It is the "multi-tool" of the ancient and medieval world, and can be adapted to suit any task. It can hold up the weary, beat off wild beasts, defend from attackers, hold up a tent, provide buoyancy in a flood, and dig a latrine. Set on fire, it can illumine the night; pointed ahead, it can cut through brambles. You can keep time with it, record information with it, draw with it, carry bundles with it, and sort stuff with it. It is the laptop computer of ancient times.

The staff is a public sign of the radical adaptability of the road runner. He or she will take any path, walk any direction, take any risk, and do whatever it takes to be with Jesus in the mission field. The "multi-tool" of the body of Christ is whatever technology or organization the road runner's imagination can create to be of practical, adaptable use in every conceivable circumstance.

3. *Wear the "sclavein."*

The "sclavein" is a rough, homespun cloak that pilgrims wear as they journey. It is humble, but technologically very useful. In hot sun, it keeps the road runner cool; in cold weather it keeps him warm. When all other clothes get soggy, it stays dry. When all other clothes rip, it stays whole. Drape it over a tree limb and you have a tent; roll yourself up in it and you have a sleeping bag.

Take what is technologically useful. Most of the paraphernalia of "church" will not stand up to hard travel. It is designed to be used once a week and locked away. Such paraphernalia is designed to help a few people do limited things very well, but it will not help a troop of pilgrims do anything that is necessary.

4. *Fill the "scrip."*

The "scrip" is a leather or cloth bag into which pilgrims put all that they need for the journey. A little food, some extra shoes, some devotional reading, whatever. Jesus had the same strategy in mind when he sent the twelve disciples two by two, except that this time he was assigning the disciples only a brief practice run for which they didn't need extra food, sandals, or tunics. Road running in their later lives demanded a few necessities.

One can imagine that each scrip will be filled with things uniquely valuable to the personality, ethnic identity, dietary restrictions, or personal idiosyncrasies of the owner. It is not possible to have generic "United Methodist" or "Southern Baptist" scrips that can be randomly passed out to every road runner. Every scrip is customized for the owner. Fill the scrip with whatever is true to yourself.

5. Choose companions.

Never travel alone. Not only is it too dangerous, but also it leads to introversion and stagnates spiritual growth. In *The Canterbury Tales,* Chaucer's pilgrims told stories to one another, humorous or sad, but no matter how trivial they seemed, they were oddly instructive. The meditations of one person soon go round in circles, but traveling companions challenge each other to grow.

However, choose companions wisely. Individuals should travel as a team; congregations in clusters of shared vision. In the latter Middle Ages, pilgrims rashly traveled with whomever happened to be on the road, and suffered brigands in their midst or cowards who ran away. In modern times, churches rashly travel in judicatories or clusters defined by geography rather than vision, and suffer brigands in their midst or fair-weather friends providing half-hearted support. Choose the companions who share your core values and beliefs, are motivated by the same sense of mission, are prepared to learn constantly on the way, and are prepared to hold one another accountable for success.

6. Sew on the "badges."

Paul frequently recounted all the places through which the Spirit had taken him in his travels. Medieval pilgrims wore badges sewn onto their sclavein: the palm of Jericho for those who visited Jerusalem, cockleshells for Santiago, St. Thomas and two swords for Canterbury, St. Michael weighing souls at the Last Judgment for Mont-St.-Michel. These "locations" might be spiritual rather than physical: St. Leonard listening to the prayers of chained captives, or a man freed from hanging represented on the emblem of St. Eutrope of Saintes.

The point is that road runners (individual or congregational) wear their story of life struggle and spiritual victory "on their sleeves" as it were. That is the mark of their authenticity, and the reason people along the way respect them. Modern traditional churches rely on "Master of Divinity" and "Doctor of Ministry" degrees, parchment certificates awarded by academic institutions hung on the walls in their recipients' studies, or various levels of training listed in their resumes. Premodern and postmodern people could not care less about these credentials! They look for the badges, the scars, the ecstatic laughter of road runners who have been there, done that, lived to tell about it, and are prepared to do it again.

7. *Learn the languages.*

Perhaps the most obvious preparation for road running is learning the languages of the people with whom you might communicate. As obvious as this sounds, many pilgrims in the Middle Ages didn't bother, and got lost. Many modern traditional churches make the same mistake. The "languages" of communication include the obvious ones of the spoken word, but also include the symbol systems in music, visual arts, bodily movement, and other nuances unique to every microculture.

8. *Respect the customs.*

This also seems obvious, but is again ignored by many would-be pilgrims. Much of the antagonism between eastern Greeks and western crusader-pilgrims in the Middle Ages resulted from arrogant indifference to understanding the attitudes, assumptions, and cultural habits of the other. Today, even if the modern traditional church is standing still, everything else is moving rapidly past them. Customs change constantly, but churches refuse to understand, and respect, the changing customs of community microculture.

9. *Keep on the road.*

One of the most frequent cautions given to medieval pilgrims was never to sleep in an inn. Stories abounded of unscrupulous innkeepers who would rob or kill travelers as they slept. More than this, the inn represented a degree of comfort that could easily tempt the road runner to forsake the journey and live in style. The same caution can be given to modern road runners, and for the same reasons. The temptation to hunker down in a lovely parish church building, or to snuggle comfortably with an affluent judicatory with large endowments can be overpowering. And although it may sound harsh, there are plenty of ecclesiastical "innkeepers" whose attentions are motivated less by the spiritual gifts and conversation of the spiritual traveler than by their income potential as members of the institution. Surely these ecclesiastical "innkeepers" would not rob or kill in order to obtain the money needed to balance the church budget, but, on the other hand, there are a lot of laity and clergy on disability!

Of course, there is a more positive reason to keep on the road. In today's cultural wilderness, it is easy to get lost. In the past, bands of pilgrims would regularly send out explorers to search for safe shortcuts, and Paul and company often diverted their journeys out of calling or curiosity, but generally speaking, it is best for the main body of pilgrims to keep to the road. A pilgrimage is not intended to satisfy personal curiosity, and road running is not about aimless wandering. Keep up with Jesus, and get to where Jesus is going. Stay on the road.

10. *Honor the Blessed Virgin.*

In the constantly changing world of the road runner, it makes perfect sense to venerate Mary, the mother of Jesus. This is not worship of a semidivine being, but a reasonable extension of the Christocentrism of the ancient and postmodern world. Shrines honoring the Virgin dotted the roads of premodern times, and travelers paused before these talismans to focus regularly on the mystery of the Incarnation (Jesus fully human and fully divine) that is the eschatological meaning of the Virgin's honorable birthing of the Christ Child. If the incognito Jesus walking the roads way beyond Emmaus is difficult to recognize, Mary the mother of God is readily accessible to the weary road runner. The symbol of the Virgin (shrine, medallion, badge, or statue) is a portal to the mystery of Incarnation, the salvation of Christ.

Shrines dedicated to the Virgin were almost always associated with healing, or with forgiveness for severe moral transgression. They celebrated gratuitous grace in its most irrational and spectacular manifestations. Who needs healing and forgiveness more than risk-taking spiritual entrepreneurs who are the pilgrims in a world of blur, flux, and speed? Theologians might meditate on the Incarnation through abstract philosophy and intellectual arguments, but ordinary people experienced the healing touch of the Christ through these talismans of grace.

Recently I was in Denver for the American Academy of Religion convention. I was walking along the affluent 16th Street Mall. Wending his way through the crowd was a rather plain-looking man wearing hiking boots, with an eight-foot wooden cross over his shoulder that he dragged along the ground. He said nothing, made no commotion, stopped at every traffic light and looked both ways before crossing the street. I laughed when I noticed he had a metal wheel attached to the bottom of the cross to eliminate friction as he walked. But then I saw him again, going up the other side of the street. An hour later I saw him again. Later that afternoon I saw him yet again in another part of downtown. I realized that the reason he had a metal wheel fixed to the bottom of the cross was not because of temporary laziness, but because he was in this for the long haul. It is as if he was, and is, and shall continue to be walking all his life.

The experience of road running and pilgrimage throughout premodern and postmodern history has revealed three long-term challenges.

The first long-term challenge is that in order for road runners to run, there must be good roads and sturdy bridges to facilitate their journeys. In ancient times, this was a task for imperial engineers and local governments. In medieval times, this was a task for local monasteries and regional nobility. In order to encourage volunteers, the local authorities would excuse people from taxes, military service, and minor capital offenses so that their hard work would count as a spiritual tithe. The good roads and sturdy bridges of the postmodern world might include well-maintained Web sites and reliable Internet connections, capital pools for mission projects and networks for continuous learning, or conflict resolution and public communications. If there is a future role for denominational judicatories in a world of road runners, this will be it. Somebody needs to maintain the roads and build bridges. The lack thereof will not stop the road runners, but it will slow them down.

The second long-term challenge is tourism. By the later Middle Ages and early Renaissance, pilgrimage had become a fashionable way to see the world. Venice (whose inhabitants were the capitalist entrepreneurs of the premodern world) even offered package tours to see the holy sites and sleep in the better hotels. Tourism and Gnosticism tend to go hand in hand, as elite and self-satisfied Christian impostors see the sites without once ever experiencing the Holy. They tour through the Christian Year, say all the right magic words at Epiphany and Pentecost, express contempt for the theologically uneducated, and sleep well. Tourism, like Gnosticism, is a lingering legacy of the modern world. It must be resisted by raising another standard of Christian living.

The third long-term challenge is the local shrine. By the later Middle Ages and early Renaissance, pilgrims had become disenchanted with the consumerism of the big pilgrimage destinations, and fearful of the dangers of the long journey. Having no desire to learn a new language, appreciate different customs, or trust strange companions, they feigned taking the cross and stayed close to home. The local shrine would do. The proliferation of local shrines—hugely popular one day and forgotten the next—trivialized the experience of road running entirely. The problem, of course, was not the distance or the hardship, but the emphasis on "shrine" rather than companionship with Jesus. When pilgrimage has a physical destination, no matter how holy and miraculous it purports to be, it ceases to be road running in the spirit of the early apostles. They had no destination in mind at all; the miracle lay in the constant companionship with Jesus.

As modernity reaches its peak of educated affluence, and as the modern traditional church drifts toward Gnosticism, the way of the Christian road runner is once again emerging as the serious alternative of Christian faith. In the catastrophic fourteenth century—a time of war, terrorism, plague, and hunger—William Langland revived the true spirit of pilgrimage in *The Vision of Piers Plowman*. The road to truth must go through the village of "Meekness" to arrive at "Conscience"; cross the river called "Be-buxom-of-speech" ["Honest Speech"] using the ford of "Honour-your-fathers"; pass by "Swear-not-in-vain," "Covet-not," and "Steal-not" and "Slay-not"; go over the bridge of "Pray-well." Once there you will find "Grace" the gate-keeper and Grace's assistant "Amend-you" ["Repentance"]. There you will enter "Paradise" by the narrow gate.[7]

The Two Choices

The choice that lies before today's Christian communities is between secret knowledge and the Way of Christ. Modern people think the choice is between the "Christian" religion, the "Muslim" religion, the "Hindu" religion, or any number of other old and newly invented religions. Postmodern people recognize, however, that the real choice is between salvation through the structures of undiscovered knowledge, esoteric rites, and the release of that spark of divinity that lies buried in every human being, and salvation through the fluidity of God's grace, the irrationality of God's intercession, and the liberation of humanity that is irretrievably alienated from God. That is the real choice.

Christianity and Gnosticism actually resemble each other on the surface, but the closer you look at them the more they diverge to be profound contradictions. Earlier I summarized the Gnostic point of view as emphasizing three things:

- Alienation from the physical world that devalues the environment.
- Obsession with the origin and significance of evil.

- Desire for exclusive knowledge of the secrets of the universe.

Gnosticism aims at a special knowledge that can be known only by an elite few, and rationed out in condescending quantities to initiates in whatever quantities the elite deem to be good for them. It is not difficult for postmodern people to see that much of the life and practice of the modern traditional church is in fact just another form of Gnosticism that competes with other forms of Gnosticism. Modern traditional churches maintain sacred temples, use terminology and practice rites unintelligible to all except the initiated, claim a theology that is, in fact, hidden from the understanding of ordinary people, and ration out grace in cubes of bread and shot glasses of wine.

The more we examine the Way and the meaning of road running, the more we see how different the Christian movement really is.

- The Christian Way is not alienated from the world, but leads into the world. It cares so much for the world as to be in conversation with it. Physical reality is not an evil that entraps the human spirit, but part of what defines and vitalizes a human being. This is why Paul goes to such lengths convincing the Thessalonians that the body itself is raised, not just a divine spark or soul supposedly trapped in the body. In Paul's view, all of created world "groans in travail," longing for reconciliation with God. The physical world is not something to be shunned because it is worthless, but redeemed because it is so valuable.
- The Christian Way is obsessed with the origin and significance of grace. Gnosticism begins with the problem of gratuitous evil, and seeks to discern a reasonable explanation through discovering some hidden knowledge that has escaped most reflective, but impure, people. The Way begins with the problem of gratuitous grace, and seeks to build a holistic relationship with

God through a simple act of faith that is possible for the ordinary person. Evil may not be understood, but it can be overcome, and there is no need to fill the vacuum between divine perfection and the human predicament with multiple layers of demi-urges and supernatural beings. All you need is God incarnate irrationally prepared to intervene on behalf of humankind.

- The Christian Way desires to know Christ, not the secrets of the universe. The verb "to know" is used in the sense of "personal relationship" rather than "analyzed databank." Christian road runners are content today to know "in part," confident that only in the end times will they "know fully, even as [they] have been fully known" (1 Cor. 13:12). What is important is not that they understand God, but that they are confident that God fully understands, and loves, them. Such an attitude strips away all egotism, elitism, and pretense of exclusivity. All can participate fully in salvation, whether Jew or Greek, male or female, slave or free, educated or uneducated, of sound mind or mentally retarded, adult or child.

As spiritualities go, Gnosticism works well when one's perception of reality assumes that enduring structures, eternal principles, rational concepts, and predictability are the foundations of the universe. In a fluid world, however, in which change, movement, relationship, and surprise are the foundations of the universe, no amount of knowledge, no matter how esoteric, will provide meaning and hope. The appeal of Gnosticism begins to fade when this different worldview becomes more broadly accepted. The best one can do is poise oneself to ride the waves of change. The "Way" to do that is Christ.

Just as traditional modern Christianity has become the official religion of the empire, occupying a place in society not unlike the temples of Jupiter and Artemis, and reinforcing the cult of Roma, so also North American churches have come to a time of choice amid the bubbling spirituality of the postmodern world. The old divisions between "evangelical" and "mainstream," "conservative and liberal," this denominational heritage or that judicatory polity, are meaningless.

Will Christian churches embrace a new Gnosticism based on hidden knowledge, elite membership privileges, intricate explanations of the order of the universe, and rationalizations about evil? If so, the Christian churches will become ever more passive, standing still to gaze at stars reflected in their own navels, and becoming increasingly irrelevant to the ordinary public. As attractive as Gnosticism was in the first and second centuries of the first millennium after Christ, it had largely perished as a serious spiritual alternative by the close of the third century.

Alternatively, will Christian churches recover the spirit of the ancient road runners and medieval pilgrims, and join in a Christian movement? The Way is based on companionship with Jesus in a world of constant change, accepts the essential incomprehensibility of life with serenity, and celebrates gratuitous grace. If so, the Christian churches will become ever more adaptive and adventuresome, walking unknown paths through the cultural wilderness, bringing welcome relief to ordinary people in all of the microcultures of the world.

Notes

1. W. W. Meissner, *The Cultic Origins of Christianity* (Collegeville, Minn.: Liturgical Press, 2000), pp. 152-59).
2. Jacques Lacarrière, *The Gnostics* (London: Peter Owen, 1977), p. 11.
3. Jonathan Sumption, *Pilgrimage: An Image of Mediaeval Religion* (Totowa, N.J.: Rowman and Littlefield, 1975), pp. 89-90.
4. Ibid., p. 91.
5. Ibid., pp. 96-97.
6. Ibid., p. 168.
7. Ibid., p. 290.

Three

THE HEART OF THE MATTER

The earliest church was one of the most vital community experiences of recorded history. Even the pagan critics of Christianity were amazed by the fervor, faithfulness, daring, generosity, hospitality, and undemanding love associated with Christian people. The attraction of the earliest church to people in all levels of social standing was that it offered the moral fiber of ancient Stoicism combined with a selflessness and optimism unknown in the Roman world. It also offered a profound, positive, personal connection with God, but without the clutter of superstition, the confusion of innumerable gods, and the burden of unintelligible rituals. Finally, it offered incorporation into a larger unity and participation in a larger destiny that transcended cross-national rivalry and cross-cultural judgmentalism, the implicit violence of which was only contained by Roman legions and deadly spectacles in the circus.

The attractive vitality of the earliest church was articulated by Christians in the simple ceremony of baptism. The most powerful witness in a pagan world dominated by slavery, and economic oppression was the ability of Christians to say (often in amazement and wonder) "I was dead, but I am alive again!" These Christians were truly alive, in whatever ways one might want to define that expression. There was something about them—a force of energy, a hope, and a restless compassion—that impressed pagan neighbors. These people were not resigned, complacent, or confused; nor were they rebellious, angry, or merely struggling for survival. They were alive!

The earliest church used two fundamental metaphors to describe its community life. Both metaphors are organic metaphors, in sharp contrast to the institutional or ritual metaphors pagans used to describe their own cults, shrines, and sacred places. What was sacred about Christian community was not a place, a floor plan, a musical instrument, or a denominational polity, nor was it an order of worship, a curriculum, or a clergy. What was sacred was a way of life. Both fundamental, organic metaphors are also clearly and intentionally "Christocentric." That is, they are centered on the experience of being in relationship with Jesus. Jesus—fully God, fully human, that incarnational paradox—was the key to this abundant life.

The first metaphor was the global vineyard. Jesus himself used parables about vineyards to describe the immanence and relevance of the realm of God for ordinary people (see, for example, Matt. 20:1-16). Notable in the metaphor of the vineyard is the clear indication that poor but entrepreneurial risk takers are more likely to be praised by the owner of the vineyard than wealthy or complacent favorite sons. The Song of Solomon, rich in its images of vineyard and harvest, was included in the earliest collections of Christian writing because the story line could easily be linked to the passionate life of Christ for his people. The vineyard metaphor is taken further by the writer of the Gospel of John in describing the mystical manner in which individuals experience the salvation of God by being "grafted" onto the "true vine" (Jesus), in order to bear fruit in the great vineyard of God (see John 15:1-17).

The second metaphor was the body of Christ. The leaders of the Gentile mission particularly favored this metaphor, perhaps because it was more readily understandable by the landless people in urban centers of all classes who had no idea how vineyards functioned and how grapes yielded wine. Paul tells the Corinthians that there is one "body," with many parts, in which the lesser members are paradoxically treated with the greatest honor (see 1 Cor. 12:12-26). The mission author of Ephesians identifies the church as the "body of Christ," one body and one Spirit, knit together and saved together (Eph. 1:23; 4:4-6, 15-16, 30-32). Another mission author quotes one of the earliest songs of the Gentile church celebrating Christ as the "head" of the "body," or what contemporary medicine might describe as the central nervous system that holds the body together and coordinates its productivity (Col. 1:18; 2:16-19).

Recently I spoke to a cross-denominational gathering of clergy and lay teams in Kansas City, Missouri. A clergyperson launched a critical tirade in the midst of the presentation about "all this talk about *Jesus*." He identified himself as a former labor organizer turned pastor, leading a struggling, small, demographically homogeneous congregation in California, which is primarily committed to social service and political advocacy. He complained that not a single person in his congregation would even understand my "key question" for church vitality, much less answer it. (This "key question" has often been repeated in my books: "What is it about your experience with Jesus that this community cannot live without?") I asked him if he himself, the pastor, could answer this question. No, he could not. More than this, he did not want to answer it. Yet he wanted his congregation to grow in vitality. The impossibility of this dream struck everyone forcibly. How can a contemporary church be in continuity with the earliest Christian experience unless Christ is the "central nervous system" of that church? Jesus, who is so central, so integral to the personal experience of church members that every sight, every touch, every taste, every sound, every contact with the world was sensitized by the vital link with him? Ideological priorities surrounded this church institution like a carapace around a beetle, a shell around a crab, or armor around a medieval knight. No doubt the beetle can chew one leaf at a time, and the crab can hide from predators, and the knight can mount a formidable charge. But they cannot "feel" or "touch" the world through that hard shell. They cannot grow unless they leave the hard shell. If they leave the shell they are vulnerable to attack or limp with fatigue, unless they grow a central nervous system once again to create agile movement and quick wits.

Heart Disease and the Body of Christ

If the missionaries to the Gentiles in the first centuries of the common era had understood human physiology in the way contemporary physicians do, they would have revised their metaphor of the "body of Christ" to be more in keeping with the other metaphor of "the global vineyard." The power of the vineyard metaphor is that as branches are grafted onto the True Vine, the organic fluids of branch and vine are shared. The life-giving "sap" of the True Vine flows into the cellular structure of the branch, enlivening every molecule so effectively that the skin of each plant literally joins together to become one plant. Christ does not function like a "head." There is no carefully considered decision. There is no carefully plotted strategic plan in this joining of organisms to become a single organism. There is simply a flow of spirit.

Much of what the earliest Gentile missionaries wanted to communicate with the metaphor of the body of Christ has the same point. Confusion about human physiology led them to associate Christ with the head, but this made it much harder to convey the deep, intrinsic unity of Christ with every part of the body. The "head" just seemed too remote from the "toes." The result was that the image of the body of Christ forced the church to think in hierarchical intermediaries that linked the head and toes of the body (clergy, polity, committee structures, and so on). Moreover, association of Christ with the head misled subsequent church leaders to imagine that spiritual life was a "head trip" (the pun being more apt than one might think). Relationship to Christ became an intellectual exercise.

The truth is that the function of Jesus in the body of Christ is more akin to the heart than to the head. It is the heart that keeps the flow of the spirit pumping to every part of the body. It is the heart that pushes the life-giving fluid of the spirit into the organic lumps of flesh known as human beings. It is the heart that converts the water that comprises the bulk of individual body weight into the "wine" that gives abundant life. It is the heart on which even the smallest part of the body is most dependent. The brain might die, and the body continues to live. If there is something wrong with the heart, the entire body, including the head and the toes, are in desperate jeopardy.

The story above from Kansas City is matched by innumerable experiences in the mission field of North America. It suggests that the real source of church conflict, church ineffectiveness, church irrelevancy, and church decline is the same as one of the most common killers of the twentieth century: heart disease.

Dr. Dean Ornish is perhaps the best-known cardiologist in North America today. His breakthrough book in 1993, *Eat More, Weigh Less* (New York: HarperCollins), was on the *New York Times* bestseller list for twenty weeks. In the following pages, I will use Dr. Ornish's work as an extended analogy to help me describe the lifestyle choices that challenge the vitality of the body of Christ. I do this for three reasons.

1. Dr. Ornish's book is not really about heart disease, but about the reversal of heart disease. Most people who are diagnosed with heart disease, or who have experienced a heart attack, feel incredible depression. There was a time when the medical community believed heart disease could be controlled, but not reversed. Dr. Ornish proved otherwise. In the same way, many church leaders give way to resignation or despair. Church decline is "an inevitable part of our lifecycle," "the result of changing demographic conditions beyond our control," or "the result of sinful indifference to spirituality in the world." Christian leaders and spiritual entrepreneurs have proved otherwise. Historic churches more than one hundred years old can be born again. Dying churches can recover to lead vital lives once again.

2. The same aging baby boomers whose eating habits and lifestyles made heart disease the leading killer of adults in the twentieth century, and who kept Dr. Ornish's book on the bestseller list for twenty weeks, also dominate most church boards today. Yet the controlling lifestyles of the "me" generation, which shaped the North American economy and global culture around their self-interest, have blocked them from recovering church vitality just as it has blocked them from recovering personal health.

   My hope is that in comparing the steps to recover church vitality to the steps to recover personal well-being, even the baby boomers on church boards will begin to finally understand the need for radical changes to the organizational habits of the Christian community.

3. Heart disease is often a hidden killer. It begins in the teenage years. Gradually the arteries clog, habits become engrained, attitudes become rigid, but for many years the individual seems to enjoy perfect health. Fewer than 20 percent of adults in North America engage in regular, vigorous exercise. The fastest growing business franchises are donut shops, ice-cream parlors, fried food outlets, and coffee bars. More than half of the North American population describe themselves as couch potatoes.

   In the same way, there are many churches with "heart disease" that appear relatively healthy. They are more out of breath when pledging the budget, but they put it down to higher heating bills. There are fewer children in Sunday school, but they shrug it off as changing demographics. Occasionally they have an "angina attack" in some ideological or dogmatic controversy, or some breakdown in pastoral relations, but once they blame the denomination or change pastors, the pain goes away and things return to "normal." Yet hidden behind these behavioral patterns lies a root cause: heart disease.

My personal health experience has been one of decades of relative abundance, along with bad eating habits, low exercise, and stressful leadership. Recently I was diagnosed with an abnormal heartbeat and partially clogged arteries. This was only discovered once I undertook a thorough stress test. For years as a consultant I have used a similar stress test with congregations. (See "The Church Stress Test" in *Facing Reality* [Nashville: Abingdon Press, 2001].) My church stress test is designed to do exactly what the cardiology stress test is designed to do. A series of thirty uncomfortable, sometimes paradoxical, but completely truthful statements function like the accelerating speed and steepening incline of the treadmill. The congregational heartbeat quickens, the leadership begins to breathe harder, and conversation around the post-worship coffee urn turns controversial. Just as with the cardiology treadmill, at some point people begin questioning the wisdom of involving themselves in such a diagnostic process! When I first used this tool, congregational stress over systemic change could be charted in peaks and valleys; some things were very stressful and others were not. Increasingly, however, congregations score off the chart in every category! Today we are seeing in the church the same desperate situation as in public health: advanced heart disease!

Conventional medical wisdom has always recommended a judicious combination of diet, exercise, and stress management to prevent heart disease or resist its advance. Dr. Ornish proved that the right combination of these three things cannot only prevent heart disease and resist it, but these three things can actually remove heart disease and restore complete vitality to a human being! His "Life Choice" program is considered by some to be radical, because it takes people from twenty-first-century diets to the diets of their ancestors, and because the "Life Choice" program is not really a program at all but a lifestyle change.

In the following pages I wish to make the same "radical" recommendation for the church to restore vitality to the body of Christ. Again using the insights of Dean Ornish as an extended metaphor, I will set out the balance of diet, exercise, and stress management that can help the church eliminate the heart disease that is killing churches by the thousands in North America today. Many will call my recommendations radical, because they require the church to return to a lifestyle of their ancestors in the earliest church. The recommendation is remarkably simple. It is not a program that can be measured and calculated, run for a length of time and then abandoned. It is a lifestyle change that does not burden people with time clocks, constitutional changes, or additional meetings, but it is a lifestyle change that is forever. It needs to unconsciously permeate every moment, every day, every week, every year of congregational life and mission.

The Vitality Diet

Heart disease among North Americans has increased sharply in the modern era, particularly the twentieth century. The simple reason is that today 40 percent of the calories consumed by the average North American come from fat (*Eat More, Weigh Less,* p. 19). Fat is a good thing in limited quantities. Fat cells function like batteries to store energy for later use. If the human body is faced with prolonged stress or famine, or if an outside force threatens the human body, that stored energy may be the difference between death and survival. However, the body only really needs 4 to 6 percent of its calorie intake to come from fat (*Eat More, Weight Less,* p. 20). For centuries this was about the limit for the average human being, until the advent of modern fast foods and luxury eating. Our ancestors were concerned about finding enough food, but today we are concerned with storing too much food and weighing too much. Our ancestors were concerned about personal, daily productivity, but today we are concerned with annual industrial productivity and stock market trends. Shorten the lunch break, eat fast food, and hurry to sit in a meeting or watch a computer screen.

One should note that heart disease is not as common among the majority of people in the world, namely, those who live outside of North America, Western Europe, and Japan. Most of these people still do not have enough food, and are preoccupied with personal productivity.

Heart disease among North American churches has also increased sharply in the modern era, particularly in the twentieth century. The reason is the same. The food modern Christian church people consume is heavy with fat. Those of you reading these lines who live in small urban, rural, or remote churches, and who regularly worry about operating deficits may think I am not talking about you. I am. Fat intake is proportionate to the size of the body, and whether you are a small body of Christ or a big body of Christ, the proportionate intake of fat is still far too high and it is killing you. Indeed, the very fact that you must worry about operating deficits every year is a sign of the disease. It is not just that demographics have changed, or that fewer people contribute their charitable dollars to the church, but that your small body of Christ is seriously ill. Stop blaming culture. Your earliest church ancestors were surrounded by even more indifference and hostility, and yet their body of Christ thrived!

A certain amount of fat in the body of Christ is a good thing, of course. It can help you survive some long droughts of economic recession and overcome periodic persecution. For example, stored financial resources and property investments can help a congregation survive months of recession and overcome unexpected persecution from the IRS or Revenue Canada. Like fat cells, these strategies perform like batteries storing up energy for future use. The same might be said of Sunday school curricula, hymnbooks, additional salaried staff, wedding chapels, and any number of other traditional church programs and tactics. Too much fat, however, kills the church. I recently encountered a century-old, downtown church with classic Gothic architecture and a concert-quality pipe organ. It also owned rental properties and had millions invested in certified deposits. The full-time church financial manager earns more than the pastor. The congregation averages fifty people in worship. These people are all Caucasians over sixty. Could there be heart disease here?

It is worth noting that Christian congregational heart disease is not as common among most Christians in the world, namely, those who live outside of North America and Western Europe. Most of these Christians lack the money to even provide Bibles for the believers, and are preoccupied with building a personally productive Christian lifestyle in the face of serious opposition.

The calorie consumption of a church can be evaluated in a number of ways, most especially by monitoring money, membership, and time.

Money

Many church leaders face operating deficits or capital expenses challenges with the avowed intention of cutting the fat out of the budget. Unfortunately, like amateurs unfamiliar with nutrition, they fail to understand where the fat really is! In the end, they actually trim away the protein, and keep the fat.

The average church consumes most of its income in the form of property maintenance, insurance, utilities, and salaries. The amount spent on actual ministries or services that change lives, grow Christians, and accomplish mission is very little. When the fat is trimmed from these budgets, it is the programs that are reduced, the continuing education allowances that are cut, the marketing strategy that is removed, and the pastor's income that is frozen.

If we could compare this calorie consumption to the budget of an early church, the contrast would be startling. The earliest Christian communities had little property, and therefore no insurance. They met in homes, workshops, and large first-floor apartments owned by Christian members and donated for the purpose of worship, fellowship, and education. Congregation too large? No problem. Just form a new Christian cell somewhere else. Some communities may have paid pastors, but most of the ministries were led by unpaid church members (including all the visiting, funeral preparation, outreach, instrumentation and singing, administration, and most of the education and worship. Therefore, an early church budget (if there was such a thing) would have been rich in protein and complex carbohydrates like training funds, mission funds, communication technologies, and specific leadership expertise. A close reading of Acts and the Epistles reveals that even financial contributions to the mother church in Jerusalem were free-will offerings given from generous hearts instead of a budget line.

Modern churches often like to rewrite their line budgets in a narrative style using phrases like "ministry of property," "ministry of personnel," "ministry of financial management," and so on. Yet these are not really ministries, but rather deposits of energy that can resource ministries. They function like fat on the body of Christ. When they are unused, they accumulate on the body, they cause blood to be diverted to maintain fat cells rather than grow mission cells, and the heart of the church labors harder to accomplish little. Rich in body fat, the church huffs and puffs to get even the minimal ministries of Christ accomplished.

Membership

Many church leaders face membership decline with the avowed intention of "building high integrity and commitment." The inability to tell the difference between fat and protein renders their good intentions ineffective. The average church merely entrenches membership privileges, uses laity until they are burned-out, and makes it even harder for newcomers to join.

1. Building integrity and commitment usually means streamlining hierarchy, not eliminating hierarchy. Control is surrendered to a few high-contributing veterans who micromanage the business of the church to make sure everything is dogmatically pure and politically correct—assessments based on their own perspectives, lifestyles, and opinions. The primary concern is to preserve a core financial base by protecting the interests of longtime members.

2. Building integrity and commitment also means extensive personality and talent inventories among the members of the church, so that the congregation can

more effectively manipulate members to use their professional talents to implement the institutional agenda. Nominations processes multiply, as do the levels of management, multiplying the fat cells of the body of Christ.

3. Finally, building integrity and commitment means burdening newcomers with additional demands for education and adaptation in order to access the life of the congregation. Baptism training, wedding counseling, funeral visitation, membership assimilation, and denominational programming multiplies for newcomers, even though church veterans are required only to serve on committees and occasionally attend worship.

If we could compare this calorie consumption to life and mission in the earliest church, the contrast would again be startling. The earliest church did not assimilate members into an institution and did not require boards to micromanage ministry. Extensive freedom was given to Christians to live within limited boundaries of values and beliefs. Higher expectations were placed on members for spiritual growth than were placed on newcomers. People offered their spiritual gifts for service, instead of burning themselves out implementing an institutional agenda.

Modern churches often like to consider themselves a "church family," describe members as "brother and sister," and liturgically pass the peace. Yet the members are not really treated as family, but as deposits of energy (money and talent) that can be tapped whenever the institution is in need. As the members multiply, blood is diverted to maintain privileges rather than welcome newcomers, and the heart pumps faster while actually servicing fewer people. Rich in statistical membership, the church labors to find volunteers.

Time

Many church leaders face growing expectations among aging members with the avowed intention of managing time well.

Unfortunately, they begin with the modern assumption that ministry is done by professionals and administration is done by volunteers. The primary role of laity, they think, is to raise money to pay others to do ministries, and to supervise those paid professionals constantly.

In the organizational models of most North American churches of any denominational polity, church administration requires as much as 40 percent of the membership to attend administration meetings. In a congregation of 250 members, average worship attendance will often be about 125, but as many as 500 volunteer-hours per month will be devoted to attending various committee and group governance and fellowship meetings. As a congregation becomes smaller, there will be a higher proportion of volunteer-hours committed to management. Leaders wear multiple hats, and the same people meet three nights in a row and all are representing different offices. One hates to burst the balloon of large churches that think they are successful, but often their church growth has nothing to do with their theology, worship, music, or property. Veteran church members flee to these congregations just because they won't have to attend so many meetings.

The actual performance of ministry is left to the professionals. This means that as the congregation manages time by increasing administration, the pastor is forced to manage time by increasing work hours. The prayer time, study time, family time, marriage time, play time becomes more and more limited, because she or he must do all the visitation, funeral preparation, preaching, worship leadership, teaching, and outreach. As more and more gifted laity burn out after subjugating their talents to meaningless meetings, these same clergy end up doing the administration anyway and stay after worship just to clean the pews for the wedding the next day.

If we could compare this calorie consumption to time spent in the earliest church, the contrast would be startling. If anyone did administration, it was probably the pastor, but there was little to "administrate." The laity, according to the spiritual gifts God had given them, did all ministries. They spent more time on spiritual matters than do contemporary Christians, and found more joy in doing it. Christian behavior and daily lifestyle were so intertwined that Christians would be hard-pressed to tell when they were working for the church and when they were working for themselves.

Modern churches like to celebrate a liturgical calendar and distinguish between sacred and ordinary time. Members increasingly speak of "going to church" rather than "following Jesus in a way of life." The liturgical calendar is not really sacred time, but a deposit of energy to be accessed whenever church leadership needs to communicate to the irregular attendees or generate a sudden rush of income. The more rigid the church becomes in observing the sacred calendar from Advent I through Christ the King Sunday, the more blood is diverted to maintain a heritage rather than relevantly share the gospel. The heart grows weary and begins to skip beats; first the summer programs disappear, then people wait until Thanksgiving to return to church, then winter mission is lost to warm vacation climates, and so on. Though rich in liturgical heritage, the church struggles for recognition in the community.

All this reveals the fat that in reality has quadrupled in modern times in the body of Christ. The financial investments, the property, the dependence on clergy, the membership privileges, the memorials, the dated but nostalgic technologies, the burdensome organizational models, the selfish use of time, and much more represent the fat in the contemporary church diet that has contributed to terminal heart disease. Jesus is not the heart anymore. Denominationalism, ideology, dogma, local history, aesthetic taste, personal privilege, nostalgia, and much more have clogged the arteries to such an extent that the body of Christ is experiencing everything from severe angina to heart attack.

Dr. Ornish offers three significant insights into fat consumption and diet that are relevant to the body of Christ. Just as human beings have tried every diet program imaginable and few have actually lastingly lost weight, so also churches have tried every denominational program and clever tactic possible to overcome deficits, increase members, reach out to more people with no lasting effectiveness.

First, "by keeping fat consumption low . . . not only do you tend to consume fewer calories, but also those calories are less likely to be converted into body fat" (*Eat More, Weigh Less,* p. 20). The human body finds it easier to convert fat calories into body fat than to convert protein and complex carbohydrates into body fat. These latter calories are more readily spent right away in productive energy. Therefore, when one consumes fewer fat calories, there is a double benefit. You weigh less and accomplish more! The same is true for the body of Christ. Dramatic reduction in the consumption of fat calories (such as property, personnel salaries, maintenance of old technologies, and so forth) has a double benefit. Not only does the church weigh less with a leaner budget, fewer statistical members, and less time connected with administration and clergy disability due to overwork, but also the church actually spends more on mission, releases more volunteer energies, and generally becomes more productive in the mission field.

Second, Dr. Ornish discovered that "the size of your fat cells may decrease if you restrict food intake for a while, but the number does not" (*Eat More, Weigh Less,* p. 22). This explains the yo-yo cycle of gaining and losing weight caused by most traditional diet plans. A program helps one lose weight, but after the program ends the weight comes back again, and worse yet, it is harder to lose the next time. A similar phenomenon happens with the church. The body of Christ adopts a specific stewardship program, membership recruitment campaign, or outreach strategy in the hope of regaining corporate health, but once the program, campaign, or strategy ends the weight returns, and it is harder to pay down the deficit, recruit more members, or do effective outreach the next time! Only when fat reduction becomes a lifestyle, not just a program, will the body of Christ truly regain vitality. The momentum shifts to vitality. The more productive in mission the church becomes, the more joyous the people of God feel, and the less likely they are to hunger for the old body weight.

Third, Dr. Ornish discovered that "when you try to lose weight by reducing the *amount* of food you eat instead of changing the *type* of food, your body responds not only by increasing the amount of insulin . . . but also by increasing your body's sensitivity to the effects" (*Eat More, Weigh Less*, p. 26). Higher insulin increases cholesterol, clogs arteries, magnifies stress, and dangerously redistributes body fat. Similarly, when churches simply try to blend their worship experiences, perform less traditional music, streamline a traditional organization, and generally try to reduce, rather than change, their behavior patterns, the body of Christ simply responds by increasing paranoia about alienating long-term members and abandoning the heritage of the church. This insulin leads the body of Christ to actually experience higher stress than if it had radically changed the diet in the first place. Moreover, it causes the body fat to be redistributed, so that ministries actually lose funding and participation, while financial management, property, personnel, and trustees receive twice as much funding, membership, and control. Transition is worse than revolution.

In order for the heart disease of the body of Christ to be reversed, more is required than just another denominational diet plan. These programs (stewardship, membership recruitment, outreach, and so forth) may be effective for a year or two, but the congregation reverts to old patterns, and returns to chronic decline, which becomes ever harder to overcome. The response in some denominations has been described as "triage." Denominations divert leadership and funding to churches that appear strong, and away from congregations for which death seems inevitable. The overall lifestyle of fat consumption, however, is not changed. The future of denominations, then, is tied to the survival of the fattest.

"Survival of the fattest" means that megachurches multiply, and that small churches perish. It means that suburban churches flourish, and downtown, rural, and remote churches languish. It means that survival depends on how much energy a congregation has managed to store up in the fat cells of the body of Christ (the financial reserves, large memberships, multiple staffs, demographic growth, and so on). Denominational regions grow smaller as leaders wait to see which congregations survive the coming rush of amalgamations and church closures, and await the subsequent redistribution of assets and leadership.

Before describing the "life choice diet" for the body of Christ, it is important to repeat the reason *why* this is so important. Christ is at the heart of every Christian community, but unless the body of Christ takes care of that relationship with Jesus, the heart will eventually fail. Christ will continue to pump life-giving blood into other Christian communities, but any given Christian community with heart disease will eventually lose heart and die. It will become physically enfeebled, endangered by conflict, and impotent in mission. In its last days, it may simply languish in bed relying on the diminishing resources of a denomination to keep it alive a few days longer in order to enjoy the intimate harmony of its few remaining friends and family members. If the body of Christ is to fulfill the quality of life God intends for it, it must recover the vitality of its relationship to the heart.

For our metaphorical purposes, there are six main food groups that human beings consume to obtain the necessary calories for life: fruit and vegetables, fiber, legumes, grains, dairy products, and meat. The simplicity of the "Life Choice diet" described by Dr. Ornish is that it does not rely on complicated measurements of food, expensive fees for program and trainers, regular trips to a twelve-step group, or a Ph.D. in nutrition. Basically, there are just three rules to the diet:

1. Reduce fat intake from the contemporary average of 40 percent of total calories, to the average of our ancestors, which was about 10 percent;
2. Eat a reasonable and satisfying amount of everything else;
3. Eat more often, but less at each meal, so that you "graze" through the day instead of stuffing yourself only two or three times a day (see *Eat More, Weigh Less,* pp. 19-26, 55-56).

Therefore, Dr. Ornish recommends that you eat lots of fruits, fiber (like beans, peas, and lentils), vegetables, and grains (corn, rice, wheat, and other cereals). Eat nonfat dairy products (like skim milk). Avoid *all* meats (including chicken and fish as much as possible), along with oils, avocados and olives, simple sugars, alcohol, and any commercial product with more than two grams of fat per serving (see *Eat More, Weigh Less,* pp. 32-33).

There are six main food groups that the body of Christ consumes to obtain the necessary calories for life: worship, spiritual growth (including all forms of Christian education), mission, leadership (including all staffing and volunteer leaders), organization (including all administration, meetings, and other governance processes), and property. The simplicity of this diet plan in preventing or recovering from heart disease, is that the body of Christ does not have to waste energy on time management, waste money on expensive denominational programs or consulting fees, waste time attending more "cluster meetings" for ailing churches, or send the pastor away for a doctoral degree in church growth. The same rules apply:

1. Reduce fat (particularly reduce dependence on property, financial safety nets, professional staffing, organ music, and all nonindigenous worship);
2. Eat a reasonable and satisfying amount of everything else;
3. "Graze" through the year instead of bunching your consumption of any one food group at only a few times during the liturgical calendar.

Many people consider the vegetarian diet of Dr. Ornish radical and unacceptable. There are variations to customize the diet to diverse lifestyles. So also my own diet for the body of Christ to prevent or recover from heart disease may seem radical and unacceptable to some. Just remember: the gate is wide and the way is easy that leads to death, but the gate is narrow and the way is hard that leads to life. Many who never imagined they could follow a vegetarian or quasi-vegetarian diet discovered that they could, and the dramatic improvement in life quality and productivity confirms their resolve never to go back.

Here is a more detailed explanation of the do's and don'ts of the six major food groups for the body of Christ.

Worship

Worship experiences are the "fruits" in the diet plan. Worship stimulates the heart. Eat all you want, as often as you want, but beware of the sugar content! Eat the fruit with a knife in a polite, orderly manner, or eat the fruit in big, sloppy bites creating a mess. *How* you worship is not as important as the *regularity* of worship. It should not just be part of the diet during Advent and Lent, occasional weddings and funerals, but every week (indeed, every day!) of the year.

However, worship is high in sugar. One must make a distinction between simple sugars and complex carbohydrates. Simple sugars not only fail to fill you up, but they leave you with a craving for more. Classical music, traditional choirs, and organ instrumentations are the simple sugars that the body of Christ dearly loves to consume. In fact, any nonindigenous form of worship (for example, worship in the cultural forms of the Christendom period between the fifth and twentieth centuries that does not utilize the cultural forms of the actual demographic groups living in your contemporary community) has now taken the form of simple sugar. Like all simple sugars, these function like alcohol and artificial sweeteners. They fill us up and send us home on Sunday morning seemingly content, and yet curiously do not really satisfy!

Certainly, at one time such music, choirs, and instrumentations were not mere sugar coating. They were complex carbohydrates. Not only was the "apple" known as worship delicious and enjoyable, but participation in such worship gave fiber and substance to daily struggle and spiritual victory. Worship can again use music, liturgy, and contemporary instrumentations to be the complex carbohydrates it is intended by God to be, but churches need to reduce the sugar coating.

Spiritual Growth

Spiritual growth is the "fiber" in the diet plan. Spiritual growth toughens and strengthens the heart. Eat all you want. Eat it daily and weekly. Eat it in classrooms with a curriculum, or eat in as fast food by using mantras, talismans, songs, and the Internet while commuting to work, walking to school, or traveling on business. This food group should be so integrated into daily life that it is like snacking on raw carrots and granola while you go about your daily routine.

There are basically two kinds of spiritual growth in this food group: children/youth spiritual growth, and adult spiritual growth. Experience in the post-Christendom world has revealed that adult spiritual growth is more important than children/youth spiritual growth. Emphasizing children/youth spiritual growth leads to short-term vitality in the body of Christ, but this vitality tends to plateau as children and youth age or as demographic changes affect the neighborhood and community. Emphasis on adult spiritual growth, however, leads to long-term vitality. It provides reliable leadership for children/youth spiritual growth and establishes a pattern and passion for Christian lifestyles that withstands changing demographics.

Within each of these two kinds of spiritual growth, there are also two more kinds of growth. *Personal growth* is often the tastiest food to eat, and for that reason it may be overdone in the diet of the body of Christ. Its natural seasoning makes discovery about one's personality, gifts, relationships, and overall identity quite enjoyable. One might say that personal growth is the caffeine of spiritual growth. *Discernment of call,* however, is also crucial for vitality in the body of Christ. It may seem excessively salty or tart to the taste, but unless this is added to the diet, the caffeine of personal growth will not have any outlet in productivity. Personal growth will quickly become an addictive dependency, in which people are forever learning more about themselves without sharing their abundance with others. Personal growth without discernment of call will lead to headaches, irritability, and sleeplessness.

Mission

Mission activities are the "vegetables" in the diet plan. Mission exercises the heart, helping it to receive oxygen, pump blood, and enliven every part of the body of Christ down to the smallest and least honorable component. Again, eat it daily and constantly. Mission should not be a program undertaken in limited quantities at irregular intervals during the year, but a daily enterprise both spontaneous and daring. There is a risk to mission that acts like adrenaline to the body of Christ.

There are basically two kinds of mission: hands-off mission and hands-on mission. The former is much less helpful than the latter. Hands-off mission involves fund-raising to pay unknown experts to do mission, or to support a charitable service unrelated to daily congregational life. It also may involve administrative oversight, occasional meetings, and policy development for social services. Hands-off mission is much less helpful, because the rush of energy and excitement in being with Jesus in the mission field is reduced. Hands-on mission is more potent. Such mission involves the actual participation of church members (alone or in teams) doing the ministries. These missions tend to be weekly or daily activities in which church members actually experience the impact of the mission on others and feel the satisfaction of laboring for love.

Leadership

Leadership is the "grain" in the diet plan. Historic and contemporary evidence demonstrates that leadership not only helps the body of Christ avoid the onslaught of diseases and viruses (unchristian beliefs and behavior patterns), but it also helps the body remain regular and avoid constipation over programmatic or ideological trivialities. Leadership keeps the body of Christ functioning smoothly, and keeps it focused on its vision and core mission.

It is important to remember that one must be judicious in selecting the best grains to eat. "Processed" grains, for example, like those found in commercial white bread or those graduated from seminaries and theological colleges, may be filled with "additives" of ideology or polity and "preservatives" of pension plans and judicatory obligations that may become harmful to the body of Christ over time. Remember, I say *may be* harmful. Generally speaking, raw leadership, raised up from within the body of Christ and unrefined by advanced certification processes is usually healthier for the church.

There are basically two kinds of leadership: salaried staff and volunteer leaders. Some denominational diet plans make distinctions between "accountable" leaders and volunteers, but this is nonsense. All leaders are accountable. The most valuable staff leaders to the body of Christ are the ones primarily deployed to motivate, train, or coach volunteer leaders to do ministries. Sometimes staff leaders are needed to manage complex mission that requires unusual expertise or government certification. Generally speaking, however, vitality in the body of Christ depends more on volunteers, particularly in all of the visitation, education, worship, preaching, and life cycle (birth, marriage, death) ministries.

Organization

Organizational activities (including administration, governance, and so on) are the "dairy products" of the diet plan. They provide necessary protein to the body of Christ that helps energize and coordinate all the mission activities of the church.

However, keep in mind that dairy products like whole milk are second only to beef as the largest source of saturated fat in a human diet. In the same way, organizational activities are second only to property as the largest sources of saturated fat in the body of Christ! Churches afflicted with heart disease not only tend to be clergy dependent and obsessed with property maintenance, but they also multiply meetings and support huge bureaucracies. In God's sight, too much organization protrudes like a belly or bulges like hips on an unhealthy church. On the other hand, low-fat dairy products in the form of streamlined administration teams, lean decision-making processes, and proscriptive administration procedures fuel and coordinate the body of Christ. (See my book *Christian Chaos* [Nashville: Abingdon Press, 1999] for further elaboration.)

There are basically two kinds of organization: hierarchical and team-based. Hierarchical organizations are typical of nearly every North American denomination and traditional church. In small churches this may be as simple as matriarchal or patriarchal governance. The larger the church becomes, the more elected offices, nominations processes, parliamentary procedure, and general bureaucracy grows. In other words, the fat tends to accumulate. Of course, in the human body there is more than one source of fat (saturated, hydrogenated, polyunsaturated, and monounsaturated). Similarly, in church organizations, there may be formal and informal hierarchies of control, divided among various groups. All of this is fat. Team-based organizations are low-fat, because they allow each cellular unit or part of the body of Christ to discern, design, implement, and evaluate mission for itself.

Property

Property and its accompanying financial reserves are the "meats" of the diet plan, and aside from clergy dependency and organizational bureaucracy the things most to be avoided. Property can provide additional protein and other nutrients necessary for the vitality of the body of Christ, but these nutrients can be obtained through other foods without the accompanying fat. Just as fish and poultry might have less fat than beef, it is possible to use more utilitarian buildings rather than Gothic cathedrals, or invest money in short-term deposits rather than multi-year certificates, but it is still fat.

The elimination of property and stagnant long-term financial reserves may strike many church leaders as impossible (just as a meatless diet strikes many North Americans as impossible). Consider, however, the countless rural, remote, and urban churches with fewer than one hundred aging members laboring to maintain traditional or historic properties all across North America today. What would happen if they sold those properties and used space in homes, apartments, business workshops, and occasional rental facilities like their ancestors did in the earliest church? Would they have more money for mission? Would volunteers be liberated for spiritual growth and outreach? Would more people be attracted to a church that would not lumber them with overhead and chronic operating deficits?

There are three mitigating circumstances that might lead the body of Christ to maintain ownership of some form of property.

1. The property is historically significant and the wider community would suffer its loss.
2. The property is an essential tactic for a particular mission to be successful.
3. Property ownership is essential to avoid the limiting influences of context or landlords hostile to the mission of the church.

Of these considerations, the first is of no importance. That may seem harsh, but God does not call the church to implement the agenda of the world. If a church property is of that much importance to the aesthetic taste or history of the world, then let the world pay for it. "As for you, follow me!" The other considerations are more relevant, because property ownership can be crucial to the success of a particular mission tactic (as newly planted churches trying to worship in public schools have discovered), or because the emerging pagan culture of North America is more hostile to organized churches (as congregations trying to rent space in community centers have discovered).

This means that although property is dangerous fat food, it may be impossible to live without it. Note again that this has nothing to do with nostalgia or heritage protection. The earliest Christians were able to do everything Christ asked them to do without property ownership, and the only heritage they wished to protect was the continuity of the mission of Christ.

All meats are not the same. There are basically two kinds of property: marketable property and unmarketable property. The former can be good, and the latter is almost always bad. This is akin to good cholesterol and bad cholesterol for the human body.

- Marketable property can be readily sold to other interests once the mission field has changed and a new ministry tactic is required. All the interior and exterior symbols are portable. The architecture of the building is not so exclusive as to deter any other potential buyer from acquiring the property.

- Unmarketable property cannot be readily sold. Its Gothic or "churchy" architecture and its floor plan (inaccessible to elderly people, parents with toddlers, and the physically impaired) make it unacceptable for other uses. Permanent symbols chronically offend potential buyers, and cannot be cheaply removed. The only value will be in the location, and the building must be demolished for the lot to become useful to the community again.

Unmarketable property is like fat that accumulates on the body of Christ that saps away energy, feeds nostalgia, and limits productivity. Maintaining such property is akin to continuing to eat pork, pastry, and fried food because Mama always taught me to clean my plate and supposedly such a diet is what it means to be a member of my ethnic group.

As leaders consider the ownership of marketable property as a tactic to control and to use in implementing a particular mission, they should consider that there are two kinds of marketable property: fixed assets and technologies.

- Fixed assets are permanent interior and exterior features, utilitarian or decorative, such as elevators, chairs, stages, small and large rooms, sports centers, and so forth. These may be necessary to a particular mission today, but they cannot be easily changed tomorrow. More important, these fixed assets are resources that do not powerfully communicate the unique core values, beliefs, vision, and mission of the body of Christ.
- Technologies are flexible, easily updated features such as video and audio systems, refreshment centers, musical instrumentation, and quality control mechanisms for light and air. These can be changed and even transported to a new site. They are used to directly communicate the core values, beliefs, vision, and mission of the church.

The Vitality Diet for the Body of Christ

Worship
Eat all the "fruit" you want, as regularly as you can. Keep all worship indigenous. Beware of "simple sugars" like classical music, choirs, and organs. Dramatically reduce consumption of these in any given worship experience to no more than the proportion of consumption among the public in your community.

Spiritual Growth
Eat all the "fiber" you can, on a daily basis, and build it into your lifestyle. Emphasize adult spiritual growth over children/youth education. Balance the tastier "personal growth" with the tarter tastes of "discernment of call."

Mission
Eat all the "vegetables" you want, every chance you get. Snack on them through the day. Concentrate on the "hands-on" missions rather than the "hands-off" missions.

Leadership
Eat the "grains" judiciously, and avoid too much "processed" leadership certified by seminaries and judicatories. Professional staff is important not in doing ministries, but in motivating and coaching volunteers to do ministries, or in managing specialized missions. Concentrate on volunteer leadership for ministries.

Organization
Eat the "dairy products" very sparingly. They are rich in fat. Abandon hierarchy and bureaucracy altogether, and eat only of "team-based" models.

Property
Eat as little "meat" as possible. Sell immediately heritage property that is relatively useless to ministry. Treat all property as changeable tactics to achieve specific mission. Choose only "marketable" properties. Emphasize "technologies" over "fixed assets." Rely on volunteer-donated space for worship, growth, and mission.

In order to reduce as much fat as possible, concentrate on marketable properties with easily upgraded technologies.

There it is in summary. The diet is really rather simple, but it may not be easy. The more overweight and out of shape human beings become, the more addicted they tend to be to fatty foods, and the more difficult it is to regain the discipline of a healthy diet. Similarly, the more overweight and out of shape the body of Christ becomes, the more it tends to be addicted to fatty foods like property, clergy, organ music and the like, and the more difficult it is to regain the discipline of a first-century church diet.

Churches experiencing advanced heart disease are often experiencing major conflict over relatively trivial issues, just as a human being with heart disease often experiences sudden anger over seemingly small things. These churches tend to quarrel a great deal, usually over ideology and dogma. They tend to be hypercritical of clergy, because their expectations are so high they are inevitably disappointed, just as heart attack patients become impatient with spouses because they cannot work hard enough to take care of the patient's needs. Finally, these churches tend to obsessively worry about losing church veterans if even small changes are instituted in program. All this follows directly from heart disease in the body of Christ.

Medical research into human health and nutrition has discovered that high-fat diets produce oxidants in the bloodstream. In medical terminology, these are called "free radicals," which roam the human body damaging human cells, hastening the aging process, and contributing to cancer, cataracts, and other diseases. Air pollution (either primary through smoking, or secondary through exhaust fumes) accelerates the production of oxidants.

In the body of Christ, we call these oxidants "controllers." Fat-rich diets combined with the damaging influences of a materialistic and competitive environment attract people who have a need to control or be controlled. These controllers gravitate to positions of power particularly on official boards, finance committees, trustees, property committees, personnel committees, and choirs, precisely those positions related to those "food groups" that are highest in fat. Controllers in the body of Christ—like oxidants in the human body—roam through the body of Christ judging, micromanaging, blocking initiative, and generally damaging the cells of the body. They inhibit the immune system of the body by imposing their personal perspectives, tastes, priorities, and opinions onto the church. Their multiplying presence leads to "spiritual cataracts" (inability to see mission), "spiritual cancer" (dangerous growths that mutate congregational DNA and sap budget, time, and energy away from God's plan toward other personal or social agendas), and other related diseases. Controllers, therefore, cause constant friction and conflict over trivialities, mission sidetracks, or unrealistic expectations of leadership. Their presence forces the body of Christ to prematurely age.

The great breakthrough of Dr. Ornish is the discovery that a fat-free diet, combined with exercise and stress management, can in fact produce antioxidants in the bloodstream. These antioxidants not only stop the progress of heart disease, but also actually repair the body so that it can regain vitality and health! In the same way, a fat-free diet for the body of Christ resists the development of harmful controllers. Some will simply leave a church that they either can no longer control or which will no longer adjust itself simply to service their personal needs. Others can be rehabilitated through higher emphasis on disciplined worship, spiritual growth, and mission. One way or another, however, a fat-free church is less likely to fight over trivialities, artificially limit creativity, burn out volunteers, or send clergy to disability. You can restore the vitality of the body of Christ!

The longer you keep a diet, the better off you are. However, at first it seems very "distasteful." There are four tastes inherent to the human body: sweet, sour, salty, and bitter. These are largely distorted or repressed by fat-rich eating, but over time the human body regains its sensitivity to the way God created food to taste. Similarly, the Vitality Diet for the body of Christ may at first seem distasteful to the church. Often churches try to claim that the diet is unfaithful to the gospel, but since this is the diet of the earliest church, that is hard to justify. The real reason churches with advanced heart disease resist the Vitality Diet is that it is distasteful to them, and arguments about faithfulness are never well grounded or even carefully considered. However, the longer the church keeps the diet, and the more earnestly it pursues fat reduction, the more the church's senses are awakened to the world as God originally intended it to be.

Here are some suggestions to help you change your diet, and stick to it!

1. Eat like a gourmet! Select what you eat, and savor every worship experience, spiritual insight, and mission accomplishment. Celebrate them, share them, and market them.

2. Avoid associating the primary food groups (worship, spiritual growth, and mission) with the secondary food groups (leadership, organization, and property). Regularly worship away from the church sanctuary and property, become more spontaneous and reduce detailed planning, and depend less on professional staff.

3. Even though denominational subsidies and professional career paths predispose the church to "eat what all of our friends are eating," deliberately analyze the denominational "banquet" and choose only those programs and resources that are more fat-free (that is, become less dependent on property, bureaucracy, and clergy leadership).

4. Create mentoring relationships with other congregations of any denominational identity who share a similar diet. The unity that you share with them is not found in the fact that you agree about everything, or come from a similar background, or even implement tactics in the same way, but that you are committed to the Vitality Diet for the body of Christ. This is your support group.

5. Avoid storing fat-rich foods like stagnant certificates of deposit, useless land investments, wedding chapels, old hymnbooks, and anything else that readily attracts controllers.

6. Eat when you are hungry, not when you feel obliged to do so. This may seem threatening, because it gives permission for people *not* to go to worship just because it's Sunday, and *not* to read the Bible just because it's Lent. Remember: fat may encourage contentment, but never really satisfies! The longer you are on the diet, the more aware you become of your spiritual hunger. People will worship more often, and read the Bible more readily, and when they do it will be because they really want to eat!

7. Eat smaller portions all through the year. Avoid orgies of spiritual interest during Advent and Christmas, combined with relatively little worship, spiritual growth, or mission the rest of the year. Deliberately trim back the feast at Christmas, and offer more food at other times of the year.

8. Aggressively invite other churches to join you in the diet. It is something to be proud of, not embarrassed about. People with heart disease often feel low self-esteem. The more you celebrate the cure, the better you feel about yourself and the more helpful you are to your colleagues.

9. Read about the experience of the earliest church in the ancient pagan world. It will help build sensitivity to your own experience in the contemporary pagan world, and give you confidence in your faithfulness to the gospel.

10. Ask the core leaders of the church to combine a low-fat diet (like the one developed by Dr. Ornish in *Eat More, Weigh Less*) with the Vitality Diet for the body of Christ. Although I have used the human diet plan as an extended metaphor for the body of Christ, the two are actually more closely interrelated. The discipline and restored health of core leaders will encourage and enhance the discipline and renewed vitality of the whole church.

Diet is only one of three disciplines required to resist heart disease and restore vitality to the body of Christ. What good is health renewal and increased energy, unless you start doing something with it?

Spiritual Aerobics

The second key discipline for resistance and recovery from heart disease is exercise. In particular, this means aerobic exercise designed to increase oxygen in the bloodstream and strengthen the heart. Other exercises may be intended to strengthen a particular group of muscles, or provide additional therapy after illness or surgery, but aerobic exercise is designed specifically for the heart. A doctor will determine a range of heart rate (for example, 114 to 144 beats per minute) and teach the client to measure his or her pulse during exercise. The exercise intensity should remain within those limitations as the one exercising builds up to, and cools down from, sustained exercise. The duration is as important as the intensity. Swimming, cycling, walking, jogging, and dance can all be forms of aerobic exercise.

The body of Christ often appears to be very busy. Church people are busy attending meetings, indulging in fellowship, fighting over issues, maintaining property, raising money, nominating offices, and providing children/youth activities. This shouldn't be considered real exercise for the body of Christ any more than commuting to work, shopping, taking the kids to piano practice, cleaning house, or playing an occasional game of golf is considered real exercise for a human being. Exercise for the body of Christ means *mission*. Mission is activity that is solely aimed at helping people other than yourself experience holistic health (physical, mental, emotional, relational, and spiritually abundant life). Mission is not what you do in and for the internal church organization, but what you do among and for the local, regional, and global general public. It is not what you do in the name of Christ, so much as what you do in company with Jesus, who is already out there in the world creating the realm of God. Mission means walking, jogging, cycling, swimming, or running to be with Jesus in a manner that is spontaneously and daringly a blessing to the entire world.

Paul was speaking of aerobic exercise when he wrote "But this one thing I do: forgetting what lies behind and straining forward to what lies ahead, I press on toward the goal for the prize of the heavenly call of God in Christ Jesus" (Phil. 3:13*b*-14). With a remarkably coincidental comparison to the Vitality Diet of the earliest church, Paul criticizes churches obsessed with internal institutional concerns eating "fat calories." "Their end is destruction; their god is the belly; and their glory is in their shame" (Phil. 3:19). The promise Paul makes is that God's power can transform the fat-rich, overweight, institutional, ecclesiastical body to "be conformed to the body of his glory" (Phil. 3:21*b*).

It will take more than just eating the right food. True health does not mean personal or corporate well-being. It means personal or corporate productivity. Your personal health is meaningless unless it benefits other people. The mere health of the body of Christ is meaningless unless it blesses all humankind. That is the difference between an amoeba and a human being, and that is the difference between a religious club and the body of Christ.

Those churches that do promote outreach and seek to do mission often do it ineffectively. They launch a program that involves a few people over a limited period of time that strengthens the muscles of one or another part of the body, but fails to really exercise the whole body. Aerobic exercise is not hard to learn, however. It requires four things.

1. Spiritual aerobics comes from the heart! The heart of the body of Christ is Jesus. Any and all mission must be done in celebrated, intentional companionship with Jesus. Many churches do not do mission in celebrated companionship with Jesus. They do good works with reference to a particular ideology or dogma. If Jesus is mentioned, it is with hushed embarrassment lest it offend anyone, or it is with legal triumph lest anyone question its authenticity. Whether Christ is invoked as a tip of the hat to a dead mentor, or as the trump card in a high-stakes card game among world religions, companionship with Jesus is the last thing on anyone's mind.

Consider the aerobic exercise class. As you run, leap, dance, and jog, you can literally feel your heart pumping. There is a mystical unity between the muscles of your body, the blood rushing in your veins, and the heart pumping rhythmically. Even the music is designed to match the beat to the rhythm of your working heart. It is this sense of wholeness that fills you with joy, and that joy is magnified when you look about you and see so many others doing exactly the same things and feeling exactly the same joy. Could you sustain this energy alone? Would others coordinate their efforts so perfectly unguided? There must be a coach at the head of the class, upon whom all eyes are fixed, one who models the moves, calls the cadence, and coaches improvements for performance.

Most church mission in North America is not of the "heart," but of the "head." It is born of an ideological perspective, voted on by a board or judicatory, paid for by obedient and often grudging pledges, and implemented by self-righteous people motivated more by a sense of duty to the institution than any genuine pleasure in blessing humankind. This is what makes much church mission so inflexible, judgmental, and so painful that most church members want to pay professionals to get it over as quickly as possible. Spiritual aerobics finds its joy by feeling the companionship with Jesus in the mission field. Like any deep relationship and great partnership, it is born of intuition, readily acted upon with enthusiasm, supported through excited expectation, and implemented by entrepreneurs.

Increasingly we hear reports from churches that have responded to natural disasters by providing support for victims of flood or hurricane. Inspired by a "just do it" attitude, emerging from a corporate lifestyle of concern for the world, supported with enthusiasm, and carried out with flexibility to get the job done, people get sweaty and dirty, and find both their physical and spiritual hearts are racing. They not only feel satisfaction in seeing victims helped and disaster averted, but also they feel a unity with strangers that is without judgment, as well as feeling the presence of Christ more joyously than ever before. That is an aerobic workout!

2. *Spiritual aerobics is sustained!* The kind of exercise that really strengthens the human heart is sustained over time. It is part of the daily lifestyle of the human being. This includes walking briskly, jogging, cycling, or running sixty minutes every day. Climbing stairs one floor up or two floors down, instead of taking an elevator, is done unthinkingly and spontaneously. One is motivated to walk two blocks to the store instead of driving not by a desire to save gas, nor even by moral objections to air pollution, but by the sheer pleasure of exercise.

Most North American churches with heart disease do mission sporadically. They devote one or two Sundays out of the year to pray for, preach on, and raise extra money for a particular mission (usually implemented by a professional missionary the congregation does not know). They devote 1 to 5 percent of their overall budget to outreach (usually overseen by a committee of people marginal to church bureaucracy who have less influence over church affairs than do trustees, finance committees, and personnel committees). These churches go about mission in the way that individuals occasionally play golf, or throw themselves guiltily into YMCA memberships every new year. However, the body of Christ that is resisting and recovering from heart disease has reversed this practice. These churches do not approach mission as a program, but as a lifestyle.

The above example of mission to victims of natural disaster is one kind of program. What makes it an exercise in spiritual aerobics is that it is simply a single moment in the sustained passion of the church for mission. The spontaneity and integrity of mission to victims of natural disaster are possible because they have emerged from a community context of vitality in the body of Christ. Denominational, government, and social service officials worry that the members of that church who spontaneously rush off to do mission might be untrained and get in the way of the experts. They do not realize that in a vital body of Christ these people have been training fifty-two weeks a year to do missions like this. They are consciously and constantly equipping themselves to do mission. They do not need to waste time authorizing it, selecting and training volunteers, and raising money, because they have been growing missionaries all year round.

Near my own hometown is a village that has become an international tourist attraction. Located at the edge of Amish communities and farms, this village is lined with boutique shops, restaurants, fresh-food vendors, and antique stores. Street musicians play old-fashioned instruments. Beer gardens serve vintage wines and microbrews. Horse-drawn carriages travel the streets. People of all ages flock here from the city. Thousands of people visit this village year round, from all over the world. In the very center of this village is a church building. It has a lovely front lawn and cement patio, yet it is a fifty-foot dead zone in the middle of the village. Nothing routinely happens on the church lawn. The only sign gives the name of the denomination, the congregation, and the pastor. The doors are closed and the windows covered. Think of the mission opportunities! The world is literally just outside this church's front door—every culture, every race, every human need passes by its front lawn every day. The congregation maintains a nice building and probably covers its operating budget, and the members likely receive great pastoral care. They hear good expository sermons, and the public is certainly welcome to attend services on Sunday morning and any other time the church is open. They probably have an outreach committee, and raise a portion of funds for overseas mission. This is a church with heart disease.

In another community near the Smoky Mountains there is a historic church not only resisting, but recovering from, heart disease. Because of its location close to shopping and huge "box stores," and being near the tourist regions of the Smokies, thousands of people travel by the church's doors as well. So they use a renovated "home improvement" center for indigenous worship through the week, open a Christian coffee bar owned and operated by church members, and run a Christian media outlet for books, CDs, and video. They deploy countless volunteers in local, regional, and global missions, and pray, celebrate, train, and motivate mission in every worship experience. Now they are renovating an old bar in the renewing downtown core in order to staff it with their own missionaries in order to become a blessing to both street people and "slumming baby boomers." Mission is a sustained exercise every week through the year.

3. Spiritual aerobics involves the entire body! The unique feature of aerobic exercise is that it works the whole body. Because the heart is the focus of the exercise, every part of the body (from head to toes) is involved. This is different from therapeutic exercise designed to help one recover from an injury or strengthen particular muscle groups. The paradox is that although the entire body is involved in the exercise, aerobic exercise actually heightens sensitivity to the surrounding environment. Exercise an injured limb, and you concentrate on yourself. Exercise the heart, and suddenly you find yourself seeing, smelling, hearing, feeling, and perhaps even tasting the environment around you. You become more aware of the people, the things, the air quality, and the events unfolding around you.

Spiritual aerobics has much the same result. Mission involves the entire body. All the members are active, including the finance committee and trustees. All the staff participate, including the secretary and custodian. Even the children have a self-perception as missionaries. Their contribution to mission may be large or small, complex or simple, but every part of the body of Christ discerns his or her spiritual gift and contributes to the mission of Christ.

Churches with heart disease deploy only a small number of people in mission. If you randomly asked members about their personal mission during coffee hour, most would stare at you blankly and a few might mention the committee on which they serve. If you ask the board members about their personal mission, most would say they were on the board because of their skill as an accountant or manager. If you ask the custodian or secretary about mission, they will say they were to just sweep the floor and answer the phone. The children articulate no desire to be involved in church life other than to learn about God and avoid embarrassing their parents. In both denominational and independent research over the past decades, marginally higher numbers of people name themselves "Christian," but dramatically fewer numbers of people do anything intentionally and regularly to be a blessing to all humankind.

In contrast, churches that are in recovery from heart disease involve all of their participants in mission. Members can readily talk about it over coffee hour; board members prioritize mission in meetings; even the custodian and secretary pray for mission, partner with volunteers to do mission, and shape their jobs around mission. For example, a semirural church in the northern Midwest involves everyone in mission in its modest-sized congregation. Members all know their spiritual gifts, and are accountable in triads to use them to benefit others. The custodian regularly trains high school dropouts as apprentices in plumbing and electricity. A team of farmers built a consulting relationship with politicians and major feed companies concerning ecological issues. By the way, the same church sent intervention teams to North Carolina to help hurricane victims, and to North Dakota to help flood victims. Make no mistake. They do name themselves "Christian"! They do it unabashedly and articulately, because they back up their claim with action.

The paradox in spiritual aerobics is that this total involvement of the body of Christ in mission actually enhances their sensitivity to their context. One might think that so much concentration on the beat of one's own heart (Christ) would draw attention away from the world. However, if the focus of spiritual aerobics is truly on companionship with Jesus (and not merely allegiance to ideology or dogma), the opposite happens. Jesus is in the mission field, so if one wants to walk with him, the body of Christ finds itself in the mission field as well. The church becomes more alert to mission opportunities, great and small, local and global. Even the smallest church sees the needs of others more clearly, and senses the yearning of others more deeply. One does not need demographic studies or expensive research. The body of Christ just knows.

4. *Spiritual aerobics is not supposed to kill you!* This last point might seem obvious, but many churches fail to grasp the significance. Mission is not supposed to kill the church, nor is mission

suppose   1. Mission not only benefits the
recipients, it also   ver.

Nevertheless, I often hear church leaders say things like "Our job is to work ourselves out of a job," or, "The mission of the church is to change the world so that the church is no longer necessary." Such thinking leads zealous church leaders to overemphasize any single mission so that it consumes all of the resources and energies of the body of Christ. The mission may or may not be accomplished, and the body of Christ becomes exhausted and dies. Such thinking has sabotaged both liberal and conservative churches. A particular cause (aboriginal rights, abortion pro or con, genetic engineering, and others) becomes more dominant than the call for abundant life itself. The body of Christ sacrifices itself for ideological agendas. The only possible parallel is that of a human being not only exercising so strenuously as to cause heart failure, but also exercising so single-mindedly that only a single present goal is achieved while sacrificing all future options.

Spiritual aerobics is not intended to kill you. It is intended to accomplish mission, and at the same time build up the body of Christ to accomplish even more mission in the unpredictable future.

Practical advice from aerobic walking or jogging can be directly applied to the body of Christ in motion. The goal is to increase the heart rate of the body of Christ; to feel Christ pumping blood into the organism; to allow Christ to give the body a real workout; to strengthen the heart of the church so that the entire body is empowered to run faster and leap even farther on the next leg of the journey.

1. *Stretch!*

Physical exercise requires stretching leg muscles before starting out, in order to avoid cramps or injury on the way. Spiritual aerobics requires the body of Christ to extend its reach beyond its normal parameters. If the mission is easily obtainable, it will not increase the heart rate of the body of Christ. Mission should always be beyond immediate grasp. It should be a stretch of the budget and a stretch of human resources to attain.

2. *Look up!*

The natural tendency in physical exercise is to look down at one's feet to avoid immediate obstacles that might trip a person on the way. Train yourself to look up. Take in the environment. Fix your eyes on the goal. In so doing, a person can anticipate obstacles well in advance, and be motivated to press on when she or he gets tired. Spiritual aerobics requires similar focus. The body of Christ tends to stare at the feet in order to avoid immediate obstacles, only to walk boldly into a dead end or lose momentum when the body tires. Look up. Memorize and appreciate the environment, and anticipate long-term difficulties. Focus on the goal of mission, or the anticipated positive results that should occur if the body keeps its momentum forward.

3. *Listen to the music!*

It is not surprising that most people doing physical exercise wear headphones and listen to music. This does not block their hearing the world around them, but provides a rhythm and a melody with which to adjust the cadences of their workouts. Similarly, spiritual aerobics is more effective when the body of Christ listens to the "music" of its core vision. Rhythm is more important than melody, because the cadence of the spiritual journey is so important. Melody may lift the spirits, but it is the rhythm of the "song in the heart" that keeps a body moving.

4. *Adjust speed through breathing and arm motion!*

Walkers and joggers learn to adjust their speed in two ways. Measured breathing can be increased or decreased, causing the walker to increase or decrease speed. Arms swinging straight forward cause the body to walk more slowly, and arms swung side to side in front of the body cause it to speed up. Increasing stride or leg motion cannot be sustained and may lead to cramps that disable the runner. In spiritual aerobics, the body of Christ relies on leadership and entrepreneurial teams to set the pace of mission. It does not rely on budgets and financial managers to set the pace of mission. When budgets and financial managers set the pace, the body of Christ "cramps" in political infighting, bringing mission to a halt. The leadership and mission teams should always be ahead pushing the limits of the budget and beyond, with financial management pushing to keep up.

5. *Avoid stray negative thoughts!*
Negative thoughts (angry memories, pessimistic attitudes, jealous feelings, vengeful images) often stray unbidden into the midst of physical exercise, resulting in an artificial and dangerous rise in heart rate. Such thoughts distract people from their goals, interrupt the musical cadence of their walks, and ultimately slow them down. Negative thoughts come unbidden into the collective mind of the body of Christ with similar results. The experience of Christ is subverted to confrontation, judgmentalism, competition, and self-denigration. Stay alert, and consciously refocus the body of Christ on the gospel of compassion, hope, acceptance, and forgiveness.

No doubt there are other bits of advice, tips, and tactics, which experienced road runners can offer to the novice just starting out on the road way beyond Emmaus. I am conscious that my own lifestyle has benefited by innumerable tips to negotiate airport terminals, bus routes, car rental agencies, the state of Pennsylvania, and the city of Los Angeles. The point is that those churches that would be road runners need to consort with other road runners, and not with churches intent on staying still.

Stress Management

In addition to diet and exercise, the third step to resist and recover from heart disease is stress management. A great deal has been written about conflict resolution for congregations, and time management and stress reduction for leaders. It is all worthwhile reading, except that most of this work ignores the fundamental issue of heart disease. What good will it do a human being (or the body of Christ) to learn the best techniques in negotiation, conflict resolution, and time management, if she or he has not previously altered one's diet and exercise program?

The truth is that when a human being addresses issues of diet and exercise, much of that which used to burden that person's life becomes much easier to bear. In the same way, when the body of Christ takes control of its diet and exercise, many of the conflicts that used to disrupt congregational life simply disappear. Congregational leaders are amazed. Their church is doing more work, expending more energy on beneficial mission, and is more active than ever before, yet the congregation is happier and the leadership is better rested. A positive attitude pervades the congregation, which makes an even more welcoming atmosphere for newcomers. The truth is that the general public intuitively recognizes ill health when it sees it, and stays away. The public also intuitively recognizes true vitality when it sees it, and joins!

On the other hand, vital living does invite increased stress. Expectations become higher. Goals become more ambitious. Risks are increased. While trivialities burden leadership less, high stakes worry them more. While minor errors are more easily corrected, major mistakes cause more serious consequences. Stress management designed to resist and recover from heart disease has four basic components.

1. Passionate and focused worship. One of the startling insights of Dr. Dean Ornish's work is the recovery of spirituality for healthy living. He speaks of meditation as a crucial strategy in the resistance to and recovery from heart disease. Why? It causes one to increase concentration and awareness of the world without and the world within, experience deep relaxation, clarify self-image, appreciate the present moment, and sense transcendence.

Worship functions in much the same way for the body of Christ. Bear in mind, I mean indigenous worship in the sense of the "Vitality" Diet. This is not perfunctory worship, although it may be liturgical worship. It is passionate, intentional worship. It has the same beneficial effects for the body of Christ as meditation does for the individual human being. Worship that models the Vitality Diet helps the body of Christ concentrate on its essential vision. It increases awareness of local and global events, as well as awareness of gifts and callings. Churches with acute heart disease tend to have either unrealistically high or low self-esteem. They tend to identify with a denomination and a heritage, but have little sense of their own limitations or potential. Worship in a vital church allows the church to accurately discern its own limitations and potential.

Perhaps the most important value of worship for stress management is that it allows the transcendent to intersect with the present. By looking either behind itself or focusing on the present moment, rather than looking ahead of itself, the body of Christ experiences that kairos of grace that strengthens and encourages it in its mission.

2. Credible grievance process. People with heart disease are often in chronic denial of their problems. This is also true for the body of Christ with heart disease. Just as human beings continue to abuse the body with smoking, fatty diets, and laziness, so also churches abuse their members by continuing hierarchical habits, nonindigenous worship, and indifference to complaints. The parts of the human body ache and complain, and the members of the body of Christ ache and complain, but neither organism has provided a mechanism to rapidly hear and respond to these complaints.

The entire spectra of potential conflict (from extreme personal abuse, to feelings of rejection, to strong disagreement over principle or program, to general dissatisfaction with the status quo) are all significant in their own right, but collectively symptomatic of heart disease. The experience of Christ is not being effectively pumped to all the members of the body. The life-giving sap of the True Vine is not penetrating through the scar tissue of the joint that is grafting outsiders into the global vineyard.

I discuss addressing discontent more fully in my book on church organization, *Christian Chaos*. Generally speaking, it is a primary stress management subsystem in the body of Christ. There are several key elements that make any grievance process credible. They must be:

a) Embedded: The grievance process must not be an anomalous program alongside the overall life and mission of the church, but should be intertwined in every activity. Every initiative must have its feedback. Every decision must be capable of assessment by the most marginal member of the church against the clarity of shared, public expectations around core values, beliefs, vision, and mission. Credible grievance processes link to constant, intentional quest for quality, and to intentional, constant, leadership review.

b) Accessible: The grievance process must be readily available to the people who know the least about the church: marginal members and the general public. Any leader in the church (including the custodian, ushers for worship, and child care leaders) should be trained to give clear and instant instructions to anyone who approaches them with a concern. Confidentiality is really just a subset of accessibility. If there is doubt about the ability of church leaders to keep a confidence, or if there is doubt among the leaders about the boundaries of confidentiality in matters of safety or legal obligation, then the process is not accessible.

c) Balanced: The three basic alternatives of discontent described in *Christian Chaos* are concerns about program, policy, or principle; grievances about unrealized expectations or activities beyond the consensus of shared values, beliefs, vision, and mission; and formal complaints about alleged abuses by leaders or members of the church. A balanced grievance process allows the church to discern which level of discontent is being articulated, and to respond with tactics appropriate to the level of discontent.

d) *Modeled:* Grievance processes are only credible if the staff and core leadership of the church visibly model them. If church leaders cannot embed the self-critique of shared values in their own lives and activities, or if they hesitate or refuse to access the grievance process, or if they cannot keep balance in discerning levels of discontent, then marginal members and the general public will certainly not participate in it. In the vital body of Christ, entrepreneurial leaders in passionate pursuit of mission cannot help experiencing discontent with themselves, with one another, and with the church as a whole. Therefore, they must model participation in the grievance process.

e) *Interfaced:* A credible grievance process for a church must interface with the denominational justice system, but more important, with the civil justice system. The days in which ecclesiastical courts could be trusted to deal fairly with significant grievances are over. Civil authorities in North America are already moving to insist on increased monitoring of the financial and personnel concerns of local churches.

Notice that "simplicity" is not listed as a key to credibility. If all five key elements are in place in the grievance process, it will usually seem simple to the participants, but this does not mean that it isn't complex or time consuming. Justice and ordinary sensitivity are rarely easy. The human body's immune system seems to work quickly and simply, but in fact the processes that discern viral infection and cancerous mutation from healthy change and creative adaptation are remarkably complex. There is work to do here for the body of Christ, and a suggestion box and an ad hoc committee are just not enough.

In the end, credibility is not a matter of legal procedure but of corporate trust. However, the latter cannot survive in any organism living in the contemporary climate of unpredictability unless the former is also in place. Metaphorically speaking, it is wonderful that the toes trust the stomach completely, but the trust will only last if the toes are confident that an immune system is working whenever the stomach makes a stupid mistake at the weekend party. It is not just that a credible grievance process can resolve intentional or unintentional injustices with integrity, but that the mere existence of a grievance process reduces the anxiety of both the members of the church and the general public.

3. Pick your own fights. Stress originates from many sources. Much of the stress is generated from within the self by the choices or habits of individuals as they experience the consequences of their actions. Some of the stress is generated by the accidents and "acts of God" that unpredictably change our lives. Notice that these stresses may be negative or positive, destructive or providential, and the healthy individual and the vital body of Christ can address them in ways described already. However, significant stress also comes from willful agents outside the self who impose their expectations upon us.

Just as healthy individuals are increasingly aware of the power to say no to outside expectations and control their own expenditures of energy, so also the vital body of Christ must be able to set its own mission agenda. This sounds easier than it is. The truth is that most congregations not only allow outside forces to dictate their mission priorities (denominational offices, secular social services, ideologically or dogmatically driven minorities, the media to name a few), but also most congregations want outside forces to tell them what to do! As individual human beings have discovered, it is easier to let the spouse, the boss, the parents, the government, the aggressive friend, the "expert," or the next emerging problem dictate how one spends time and energy. These individuals end up fighting battles not of their own choosing. The body of Christ has a similar problem.

The more the body of Christ takes control of its own diet and exercise, the more authority it also will take over its own mission agenda. This is why discernment processes that build clarity and consensus about shared values, beliefs, vision, and mission have replaced old-style strategic planning among organizations of all kinds in North America (see my book *Moving Off the Map* [Nashville: Abingdon Press, 1998] for one such process). It allows the body of Christ with integrity to say no and resist outside pressure. "This issue may indeed be important, but it is not *our priority* at this time." When outside forces then try to coerce it to adopt a foreign agenda, it is empowered to differentiate its own identity and declare its own purposes.

Insisting on your right to choose your own battles may in the short term *increase* stress. Outside forces such as those named above are remarkably persuasive, and sometimes quite nasty, in manipulating churches to serve their purposes. In the long term, however, the integrity that is generated builds confidence.

This is not to say that the body of Christ should become insensitive to prophetic voices beyond the church, but simply to recognize that prophetic voices influence the church by speaking to the "heart" of the body of Christ rather than by manipulating ecclesiastical agendas. When the body of Christ experiences heart disease, its deep spirituality and clarity of mission are all compromised, and the only way to get its attention seems to be to coopt its strategic planning. Over the past forty years, one may have learned from the demise of the Civil Rights movement that this doesn't work. Some results are gained, but the body of Christ dies of heart failure, and without energy to maintain success, society reverts to its original destructive habits.

Choose to fight your own battles. This means that the body of Christ must work hard to build its own sense of integrity (behavioral expectations, beliefs to die for, visions that inspire, mission goals), and to articulate that integrity through spontaneous deeds and daring risks.

4. Shift your mental model. Most churches, great and small, in North America at the beginning of the twenty-first century have adopted a mental model foreign to the earliest church, which is based on the concept of "church family." Perhaps this is because today marriage and family life seem to be breaking down, and the people want to prioritize personal relationships and children/ youth ministries. Perhaps this is because homogenous culture seems to be breaking down, and people want to identify with a tribe or subculture. Whatever the motivation, the mental model of church family encourages the church to have unrealistic expectations of harmony, which have become increasingly fragile in the emerging pagan world.

It is true that the earliest Christians often referred to one another as "brother" and "sister," and there is at least one occasion in which Paul (or a disciple of Paul) urged Christians to work for the good of all and especially "for those of the family of faith." However, the notion of brotherhood or sisterhood and family that lies behind these texts is shaped by ancient Roman understandings of family ties, and not by twenty-first-century assumptions about the nuclear family of Mom, Dad, and the kids.

- The earliest church used the metaphor of "family" to describe obligation, not membership. When followers seek to convert his ministry into a family affair, Jesus says "whoever does the will of God is my brother and sister and mother" (Mark 3:35). Ancient Roman culture understood "family" as a network of obligations and duties, not as the sum of people living under one roof (or steeple). This is reinforced when Jesus refers to all the "outsiders" (the hungry, thirsty, naked, imprisoned, and sick *strangers* of the world as his true "brothers and sisters"). In this ancient context, statements that jar the sensitivities of twenty-first-century "church families" that are similar to Jesus' rebuke of the disciple wanting to first bury his parent are quite understandable: "Follow me, and let the dead bury their own dead" (Matt. 8:22).
- The earliest church used the metaphor of "family" to describe universal inclusion, not tribal exclusion. That really is the whole point of Paul's letter to Philemon, in which he tactfully explains that the escaped slave Onesimus is an equal and beloved brother in Christ and

not someone else's property. We are family in the sense that all humanity has been adopted into a network of obligation. In Roman fashion God the Father has but one son and heir (Jesus), but in a fashion scandalous to Roman custom God has then adopted the rest of the world to be fellow heirs of abundant life (Rom. 8:28-30). Hence, the family is not a tribe whose identity is based on excluding others by certificates of membership, but a predetermined and scandalous act of God that has included everybody. Thus, Paul writes that there is no longer slave nor free, male nor female, Jew nor Greek, but "all of you are one in Christ Jesus" (Gal. 3:28).

- The earliest church used the metaphor of "family" to describe a community of faith, not a family of origin (Gal. 6:10). The common thread of communion with Jesus was the only way they could distinguish themselves from the cultic, tribal, or nationalistic thinking of the Roman world that worried obsessively about birthrights. The term "family" has exactly the opposite meaning for churches in contemporary North American culture. Churches explicitly mean "family *of* origin" by emphasizing denominational heritage, and implicitly celebrate "family of origin" by maintaining their cultural or demographic homogeneity. The "family members" all look remarkably alike. The "family of faith" in the New Testament were remarkably diverse, the only common trait among members being relationship with Jesus celebrated through baptism.

Theoretically, it is possible to maintain the mental model of "church family" to describe the identity of the church, but the discontinuity between what early Christians meant by family and what contemporary North Americans mean by family is too great for practicality. It leads to inevitable and unnecessary stress because the behavioral expectations of individuals and group are so contradictory.

This stress is most clearly visible when a contemporary, traditional church family addresses conflict. They worry obsessively about splitting the church, and experience high anxiety over losing any individual from membership. The admonitions of Jesus become incomprehensible and frightening to the modern church family. Jesus says:

> If your right eye causes you to sin, tear it out and throw it away; it is better for you to lose one of your members than for your whole body to be thrown into hell. (Matt. 5:29; see also Matt. 18:8-9)
>
> For if you love those who love you, what reward do you have? . . . And if you greet only your brothers and sisters, what more are you doing than others? (Matt. 5:46-47)
>
> If another member of the church sins against you . . . take one or two others along [as witnesses]. . . . If the member refuses to listen . . . let such a one be to you as a Gentile and a tax collector. (Matt. 18:15-17)

Such admonitions are incomprehensible to the modern understanding of family. However, these admonitions are quite understandable if the family is understood in the context of Roman culture and the earliest church.

The mental model that reduces stress is the combination of True Vine and Body of Christ that I have suggested here. These metaphors predominate in the earliest church, because they describe more effectively the organic nature of the Christian community, and place clear emphasis on the Christocentric "heart" of congregational life.

Most stress is insidious—hidden, unrelenting, lurking beyond the consciousness of even the most self-aware individual. The stress that really disables the body of Christ is not open conflict, or complaints emerging through a grievance process, or even warfare over worship and music. It is the more insidious stress of feeling that powerful forces lie in wait to ambush the mission, or that mission failure might lead to self-destruction, or that imagined evils might sabotage a church's best efforts. It is the escalating speculations about "What if . . . ?" and the unarticulated fears about personal or corporate inadequacy. The solution is not simply to become more self-aware, but to network with like-hearted partners who can both critique and reassure one another.

Images of pilgrims in ancient and medieval times often show "demons" or "tempters" lurking in the background. This is the insidious stress that constantly hampers the road runner's journey. Today's road runners can adapt the following coping strategies, based on the examples of earlier pilgrims:

- *Travel with companions:* The members of a cell, small group, or traveling company support one another. They can exhort, rebuke, coach, and encourage you to discern the "demons" that dog your corporate travel as the body of Christ. These companions are not linked by such external things as proximate location to one another, church size, or even comparable demographics, as is the case in modern traditional denominational judicatories. They are linked by compatible values, beliefs, vision, and mission.
- *Focus on incarnation:* It is the mysterious, saving presence of God incarnate (fully human and fully divine) that repels the demons by renewing conviction in acceptance, forgiveness, and unending love. This is why pilgrims venerate the Virgin Mary, celebrate Christmas most passionately, and look for Christ incognito in the face of every beggar or passerby. They do these things "religiously," constantly, repetitively, perhaps even liturgically. Perhaps they keep their focus by using talismans of prayer beads, shrines, and symbols that are all intended as constant reminders of the moment-to-moment incarnation of Christ.

The legend of Faust originated in early Christian experience as the story of Theophilus, the steward of a bishop in Cilicia, who wanted to succeed his master on the episcopal throne. He sold his soul to the devil in exchange for the knowledge and power to accomplish his goal. Diverted from the Way, a contract was written and signed, and Theophilus gained all that he coveted. Later he experienced intense remorse. He prayed night and day for deliverance he knew he did not deserve. The Blessed Virgin miraculously intervened, snatched the contract from the devil, and restored Theophilus to the Way of Christ. This is the ultimate stress-reducer: having confidence in the salvation even of those who deserve to be damned.[1]

Leaders Lead!

Both Gospels and Epistles return to the mental models of True Vine and Body of Christ over and over again. Most Christians are familiar with Paul's remarkable insight into the metaphor of the "body of Christ" in which he observes that the "least honorable parts in fact receive the most honor" (see 1 Cor. 12:23, 24). If Paul were addressing contemporary Christians with further insight into the congregational metaphor of human physiology and heart disease, he might well add that the parts of the body who receive the most honor are the ones who must work hardest to model the virtues of spiritual vitality.

In order for the body of Christ to resist and recover from heart disease, the leaders of the church must work harder at the remedy. They are the ones who are most disciplined about the Vitality Diet, the ones who are most energetic about spiritual exercise, and the ones who are most intentional about stress management. In a sense, it does not matter what particular skills leaders possess, only that they are most visibly earnest about diet, exercise, and stress management. Church members may be allowed to deviate from the diet, relax from exercise, or divert their minds with extraneous worries to some degree, but the leaders must be the most rigorous. They are the models—the aerobics instructors— the most clearly focused missionaries of the body of Christ.

Earlier I summarized the "Vitality Diet" for the body of Christ. How would that fat-free diet be implemented among church leaders, and how does that contrast to their current fat-rich consumption?

Vitality Diet

Worship
Leaders eat large quantities of "fruit," both corporate worship and personal prayer. They avoid "simple sugars," and seek God in indigenous cultural forms that may even offend their aesthetic tastes.

Property
Leaders avoid "meat." They refuse to finance inefficient heritage properties useless to mission. They upgrade to current technologies; protect the marketability of any properties; minimize overhead.

Spiritual Growth
Leaders eat lots of "fiber": Bible study, constant learning in any and all topics, disciplined reflection and theological conversation. They balance personal growth and meditation about call.

Organization
Leaders avoid "dairy products": (meetings, hierarchies, and bureaucracies). They encourage entrepreneurship, train leaders, coach teams, and practice "letting go." They concentrate on "boundaries," not "tasks."

Mission
Leaders eat "vegetables." They research and implement mission beyond the church. They "snack" through the week seeking spontaneous ways to bless non-church people. They motivate others in mission.

Leadership
Leaders eat "grains" judiciously. They avoid politically correct or trendy continuing education, and improve relevant mission skills. They focus on multiplying more volunteers for ministries.

Current Fat Diet

Worship

Clergy rarely eat "fruit." They coordinate worship, but do not really worship. They give little time to serious prayer or devotions, are too tired for meditation, devour "simple sugars" in nonindigenous cultural forms.

Property

Clergy eat too much "meat." They spend way too much time protecting heritage, administrating "fixed assets," maintaining old technologies, addressing operating deficits, and celebrating lack of marketability.

Spiritual Growth

Clergy talk about "fiber," but rarely eat it. They curtail continuing education and are "too busy" for serious reflection and conversation. They worry about time management, but rarely reflect on their original calling.

Organization

Clergy eat too much "dairy." They spend huge amounts of time attending meetings (administrative and program planning), maintaining or building power, servicing hierarchies and bureaucracies.

Mission

Clergy eat too few "vegetables." They worry obsessively about keeping members happy; spend most time among members, avoid culture, "snack" on nonindigenous music, motivate little outreach.

Leadership

Clergy eat "grains" recklessly. They are too concerned about "correctness" and protecting pension and career path. They are caught up in prestige and the need to be loved. They are obsessed with professional control.

You will notice in the comparative charts above that the current fat-rich diet of church leaders (especially clergy) is exactly *the opposite* of the Vitality Diet. Like Paul bemoaning his sinfulness, church leaders need to awaken to the sad reality. "The things that I do, I do not want to do; and the things that I do not want to do, are the very things that I do!" Like Paul, church leaders might well exclaim "Wretched man that I am! Who will rescue me from this body of death?" (Rom. 7:24). The answer, of course, is to focus on the heart and lifeblood of the body of Christ. "Thanks be to God through Jesus Christ our Lord!" (Rom. 7:25).

Of course, not a few clergy and church leaders are in chronic denial about their heart disease. Comparing the "diets" above, they fool themselves into believing their food choices are sound. Asked if they exercise, they offer platitudes about the world being their parish and assure themselves about their interest in mission. Asked about their levels of stress, they give warm smiles of reassurance, confident that discontent can be readily voiced and effectively heard in their churches, that their boards are in tune with God's mission, and that the harmony of the church family is prized. The truth is hard to accept:

- Examine what they actually do during the week, and you discover they spend little time in prayer, spiritual growth, and hands-on mission motivation beyond the church, and they expend extraordinary energy honoring membership privileges, taking care of church insiders, serving bureaucracy, overseeing staff, and maintaining property and high-overhead budgets.
- Shadow them through the week, and you discover just how little exercise they really get. What little they actually do in regard to mission exercises a program or a committee, but not the heart of the church. It is rarely sustained beyond a few weeks. It primarily involves fund-raising and property use, but relatively few volunteers. It is often in response to some prompting from an authority beyond the body of Christ.

- Monitor their stress over the week, and you discover that their lack of proper diet and quality exercise have made them vulnerable to all the trivial complaints of increasingly needy members. They rush about seeing to unimportant matters. No credible grievance process exists apart from "trusting the clergy," and an aging congregation of diminished numbers worries the leadership more and more. Their mission is, in fact, controlled by powerful matriarchs or denominational policies. Their mental model satisfies contemporary pagan culture, but is foreign to ancient Christian experience.

The good news is that increasing numbers of clergy and laity simply refuse to live like that anymore. They are looking for serious, long-term remedies. They long for joyful vitality.

Cardiology specialists discover that many modern people (especially executives, professionals, and health care workers) refuse the life choice diet. They complain that they could not possibly do it in their contemporary context. They scoff that it is unrealistic, absurd, and totally incompatible with their important obligations and urgent priorities. Curiously, doctors, nurses, and health care professionals are among the first to complain! Their complaint is undermined, however, by the fact that increasing numbers of people are doing it, and that this discipline is making them more productive and not less productive. Their scoffing is challenged by the high rates of death, disability, changed career paths, broken marriages, and substance abuse that are the side effects of their inability to change.

The same experience is true for those who try to help congregations see their unhealthy habits and behaviors. Congregations and congregational leaders constantly refuse the Vitality Diet for the body of Christ. They complain they could not possibly do it in their contemporary context. They scoff that it is unrealistic. Strangely, it is the clergy, denominational leaders, and longtime veteran laity who scoff the most! They are just too busy, their present priorities are just too important! Sometimes they say "Yes, I'll do it, but I'll start after the busy season of Christmas," "I'll start this summer when I have more time," or "I'll start after the capital campaign has resolved our financial problems." One crisis will succeed another, the fresh start chronically postponed, and these leaders will never realize that the reason they are in chronic crisis in the first place is that they have heart disease!

The complaints of clergy and veteran church people are increasingly undermined by the fact that increasing numbers of church leaders and congregations are in fact doing it! "Heart disease" in the body of Christ is not only being resisted by a new species of church emerging among both former liberal and conservative camps, but one also finds that traditional and historic churches are actually reversing heart disease and finding new vitality. The side effects of heart disease are already evident among church leaders: high rates of death, disability, changed career paths, broken marriages, and substance abuse. Yet the joys of healthy vitality are also visible among those leaders and congregations who have chosen a radical, but ancient remedy.

Note

1. Jonathan Sumption, *Pilgrimage: An Image of Mediaeval Religion* (Totowa, N.J.: Rowman and Littlefield, 1975), pp. 275-76.

Four

"O BROTHER, WHERE ART THOU?" (QUO VADIS?)

In an ancient legend first recorded in the "Acts of St. Peter," and later repeated by Ambrose, that paradigmatic road runner Peter fled persecution in Rome along the Appian Way. As he left Rome, he encountered the risen Christ coming from the opposite direction. A long, long way beyond Emmaus, Jesus was on his way to Rome. *"Domine, quo vadis?"* Peter asks. "Lord, whither goest thou?" Jesus answers: "I am coming to be crucified again." Hearing this, Peter immediately turned around and returned to Rome, where he himself was martyred. The Church of S. Maria delle Piante marks the place of Peter's grave.

In 1896, Nobel Prize winner Henryk Sienkiewicz published the novel *Quo Vadis*, and in the 1950s Hollywood created the film version, but both modern retellings miss the essential point. Modern traditional Christendom tells the story as if decadent, violent, ignorant pagans gratuitously slaughtered civilized, intelligent, nice people whose only fault was to worship one God. The actual point of the legend is much more critical of contemporary people. Refined, peaceable, intelligent pagans quite understandably attacked a Christian "Way" that fundamentally contradicted their orderly, structured, and highly spiritual world. The offense of the Way was that it was not a data bank of knowledge of politically correct and dogmatically pure information, but a lifestyle of constant companionship with a resurrected wanderer, Jesus. If only those early Christians would have just settled down, founded temples, and invested their energy in Sunday schools, they would have fit right in. But they didn't. They kept moving around, subtly turning the world upside down.

In 2000, Joel Coen and Ethan Coen released a truly postmodern film with ancient connections called *O Brother, Where Art Thou?* It was a contemporary remake of Homer's *Odyssey* that raised a similar question to *Quo Vadis* in an inverted sort of way. It is as if Christ and Christendom have encountered each other once again on a road way, way beyond Emmaus (this time on a dirt road in Depression-era Mississippi), but this time it is Jesus who asks the modern, traditional church: *O brother* (or "sister"; by all means, let us be inclusive in this, too!), *whither goest thou?*

True to the epic of Homer, the hero of this movie is Ulysses Everett McGill, former small-time embezzler and current escaped convict, a true representative of modern people. He is quick-witted, well educated, and charismatically persuasive, but his first thought in a crisis is to protect his hairdo rather than the lives of his comrades. He creates the illusion of being a profound person, but is a good deal less insightful and courageous than he thinks. Like any good Gnostic, he and his fellow convicts are trying to escape the chain-gang existence of this world to recover a "treasure," the location of which is Ulysses' own secret knowledge. Unfortunately, or providentially, for Ulysses (depending on how one looks at it), Fate has placed him on the brink of the postmodern world.

Fate comes in the guise of a blind railroader pumping a rail inspection car. The man has no name and appears to be going no place in particular.

> You seek a great fortune, you three who are now in chains. You will find a fortune, though it will not be the one you seek. But first…first you must travel a long and difficult road, a road

fraught with peril. . . . You shall see thangs, wonderful to tell....I cannot tell you how long this road shall be, but fear not the obstacles in your path, for fate has vouchsafed your reward. Though the road may wind, yea, your hearts grow weary, still shall ye follow them, even unto your salvation.[1]

True to prediction, there is no buried treasure, and the secret knowledge proves groundless. All of Ulysses' supposed education, wit, charisma, and courage is revealed empty. The real fortune he finds is the road itself, the companionship on the road, and a final encounter with Christ in which Ulysses discards his pride, prays to God, faces inevitable and well-deserved doom, and finally, *finally,* thinks of the lives of his companions *without* worrying about his hairdo.

What happens when Homer's Odysseus meets traveling Jesus way beyond Emmaus, or when Ulysses Everett McGill meets the incognito Christ along a railroad track in Mississippi? The premodern and postmodern worlds are changed. The classical legend of Odysseus ends with the hero returning home, tricking his way into the pre-wedding banquet of his wife Penelope who thinks him dead, slaughtering all the would-be suitors, and living happily ever after. That would be how the modern version would end as well. The action hero would become the "terminator" for all the hypocrites and evildoers. When Jesus meets the postmodern world on the road, the plot changes.

Ulysses Everett McGill does not save himself and there is no bloodbath. A miracle saves him and there is a rather radical baptism. It is really quite irrational and beyond explanation, even by the most esoteric knowledge. At the very moment of his doom, the valley is flooded to power a hydroelectric dam, and all is swept away. In the last scenes, the well-ordered, structured, modern world has been swept away by the fluidity of postmodern experience and the overwhelming grace of God. The journey continues, only this time underwater.

The Christian legend of *Quo Vadis* hijacks the Homeric legend of *Odysseus.* What really ties *O Brother, Where Art Thou?* to the ancient *Quo Vadis* legend is the oft-repeated theme song "I Am a

Man of Constant Sorrow." It doesn't really fit Odysseus. He is a man of frequent misfortunes who finally wins in the end. Jesus is the "man of sorrows, familiar with suffering" (Isa. 53:3 NIV) who "took our infirmities and bore our diseases" (Matt. 8:17). It is not difficult to connect Jesus on his way to yet another cross, with Ulysses and his friends Pete and Delmar who sing this song about themselves as the unlikely trio known as "The Soggy Bottom Boys." It is even more significant that it is this christological song that captures the wildly enthusiastic attention of every ordinary person in the state of Mississippi and the Mediterranean world, *except* for the state police and secret societies like the Ku Klux Klan.

I am a man of constant sorrow; I've seen trouble all my day.
I bid farewell to old Kentucky, the place where I was born and raised.
> (The place where he was born and raised.)

For six long years I've been in trouble, no pleasures here on earth I found.
For in this world I'm bound to ramble, I have no friends to help me now.
> (He has no friends to help him now.)

It's fare thee well my old lover, I never expect to see you again.
For I'm bound to ride that northern railroad, perhaps I'll die upon that train.
> (Perhaps he'll die upon this train.)

You can bury me in some deep valley, for many years where I may lay.
Then you may learn to love another, while I am sleeping in my grave.
> (While he is sleeping in his grave.)

Maybe your friends think I'm just a stranger, my face you'll never see no more.
But there is one promise that is given, I'll meet you on God's golden shore.
> (He'll meet you on God's golden shore.)[2]

Don't be misled by references to Kentucky instead of Palestine, or to six years instead of two millennia. This is the traveling Jesus, all right, and you see the essentials in the refrain and in the *Kerygma* of Christian road runners as they pass through Philippi[3]:

- He's left the place where he was born and raised;
- His would-be friends have abandoned him or have yet to catch up;
- He dies on every train, in every human context, for every person;
- His death is but an illusion;
- He will meet you again, once we all catch up, on God's golden shore.

It may be difficult for the relatively wealthy, prestigious, property-owning, clergy-privileged church institutions that represent the established religion of the present empire to ever compare themselves to The Soggy Bottom Boys, but that is exactly what has to happen if the Christian community in the twenty-first century is to be revitalized. Join Paul, Peter, Lydia, Priscilla, and all the road runners and rediscover the Christian *movement.*

This is the song of Jesus, sung way beyond Emmaus. It is the song of ordinary spiritually hungry, downtrodden people. Both gospel truth and welcome relief, the song offers an alternative to the Gnosticism of modern times. Salvation does not lie in hidden knowledge yet to be discovered by science or in supernatural magic. Salvation lies in a Way of Life, running the road, way beyond Emmaus, Rome, and Mississippi in companionship with Christ. You will indeed catch up with him on God's golden shore.

This has been both an easy and a difficult book to write, and I suspect it has been both an easy and difficult book to read. It is easy because the realities of the contemporary pagan world and the status of the established denominational church as the official religion in the pagan world are so obvious. It is difficult because these realities make us so painfully aware of how far the Christian church has departed from the apostolic Christian movement that spread from Jerusalem to Samaria, Antioch,

Ephesus, Philippi, and to the ends of the earth. The heart of the matter is Jesus. Either Christian churches do not really know what it is about their experience with Jesus that their communities cannot live without, or they do not really want to be with Jesus on the road to mission.

Either way, the pagan public does not care about the Christian church. At best, the pagan public wants to keep the shrines of official religion open so that it can perform rituals and consult auguries whenever the welfare of the state and the status quo of privilege are threatened by terrorist attack or Carthaginian invasion. At worst, the pagan public views Christianity with the sentiment of Suetonius as "a novel and mischievous superstition."[4]

The vitality of Christianity in North America depends upon its becoming a *movement* again. The church is not a "family," but a "body," a living organism. This body is experiencing "heart disease" because it stresses itself by debating ideological and dogmatic trivialities, living on a high-fat diet, and never, ever, getting exercise. Churches are bodies at rest—"couch potatoes" watching mission on TV, consuming heritage property and bureaucracy like potato chips, and quarreling over the remote control.

Recovery from heart disease will require a radical lifestyle change. Joggers understand the sweat required to have a healthy heart. Paul, Silas, Priscilla, and all the apostles understood that the only way to recapture true spiritual vitality was to follow Jesus on the road to Emmaus and beyond. We are right back to where the apostles were traveling the Roman roads and waterways. Pack your tools, an extra change of clothes, a little food for the journey, and embark on mobile mission.

- Carry a transformational experience to every pagan passerby.
- Narrate the story of Jesus.
- Invite people into extraordinary companionship whenever you stop on the way.
- Model an alternate lifestyle.
- Act as if there is not a moment to lose.

Christianity is a mission movement, not an institution. Don't worry about what you will eat or how you will dress, because the God of transient creatures will take care of you. Don't lag behind trying to bury your dead heritage decently. Don't bother to pack a handbook of denominational polity or burden yourself with bars of gold and useless capital funds. Just put on your running shoes and hit the open road. Jesus is already there.

> I want to know Christ and the power of his resurrection and the sharing of his sufferings by becoming like him in his death, if somehow I may attain the resurrection from the dead.
> Not that I have already obtained this or have already reached the goal; but I press on to make it my own, because Christ Jesus has made me his own.
>
> (Paul to Lydia and the other church leaders at Philippi, during his imprisonment in Rome, Phil. 3:10-12)

Notes

1. *O Brother, Where Art Thou?* Touchstone Pictures, 2000.
2. Dick Burnett, "I Am a Man of Constant Sorrow."
3. Compare Philippians 2:5-11.
4. Quoted by James S. Jeffers, *The Greco-Roman World of the New Testament Era* (Downers Grove, Ill.: InterVarsity Press, 1999), p. 22.